D1378747

**Civic Garden Centre
Library**

The Flower Arranger's Year

The Flower Arranger's Year

Jane Derbyshire

COLLINS

For Phil
who can build conservatories
and such delights

Martin Rice photographed the flower arrangements

Other photographs by the author

Line drawings by Vana Haggerty

Edited and designed by The Nassington Press
assisted by Safu-Maria Gilbert

© Madge Green 1981

First published in 1981

Published by William Collins Sons and Company Limited
London Glasgow Sydney Auckland Toronto Johannesburg

Printed in Great Britain

ISBN 0 00 411655 0

Contents

INTRODUCTION

In winter, when the fields are white,
I sing this song for your delight —
In spring, when woods are getting green,
I'll try to tell you what I mean.
In summer, when the days are long,
Perhaps you'll understand my song;
In autumn, when the leaves are brown,
Take pen and ink, and write it down.

Lewis Carroll

As you turn into the rough lane, off the hilly road which comes wandering up between the fields from the town, you can see, a little way along, a low, brown, oddly-shaped wall with a pale gleam of yellow peeping over. Even on blustery winter nights when the lane is dark, lit only by the lamp under the wild holly bush on the corner, the gold is still there. It makes, I hope, a small, cheerful wave of welcome for those who travel home along it, as their car headlights pick it up for a moment. The warm, friendly colour comes from a gold-yellow ivy called 'Buttercup'.

It is one of a number of different ivies I set some years ago to scramble up and over the wall which edges the old farm lane at the front of our small country house with its blue-green colour-washed walls. In spring the ivy arches over sweetly-scented wallflowers. In summer, as the wild dog roses come to flower and the unmade lane gets a bit dusty, it bends to meet cottage garden valerian, and as the small red crab apple sets fruit against wide sunny skies it makes a perfect setting for hollyhocks.

But the point of mentioning this handsome ivy is that it leads me straight into what this book is really all about. I have a strong belief that plants and flowers and growing things, and spreading the happiness of them, are particularly important in our plastic-enfolded and over-busy lives today. And that, as people who like flowers, we could extend our use of them in far more vigorous, imaginative, outward-looking ways than perhaps we do. I know we are all busy, most of us work, we come home tired with the pace of life, and many people feel that the world is changing so fast that the ordinary person can really have small influence upon it. Yet we who love flowers could do a great deal with them and through them to make life in general more pleasant. The world need not be a jungle – it can be a garden!

I too lead an over-full life as a journalist, lecturer, and national judge and adjudicator in flower arranging. I am married, have a home to run, serve on various committees, have many friends, garden through the year, grow houseplants, 'do' interviews and photography, collect books, and so on, I could go on for ever!

However, I find that wherever I go and whatever I do, no matter how tiresome the day, flowers are a never-failing refreshment and cheer, a splendid back-up at all times and in everything. I often have to be away from home on some small adventure or other, perhaps an assignment involving meeting a strange man at the end of Ryde Pier on a February afternoon, as I had to do last year, lunching with a star in March, meeting a TV personality at home in July, or talking to some ordinary person who has done something extraordinary, at any old time. Wherever I go I always try to take a small posy of my garden flowers along with me. Rich and poor, famous or unknown, people immediately warm to the flowers; they smile, the ice is broken, we relax, we like each other.

Flower arranging and growing things are twin pleasures running easily together for me, each naturally supporting the other. In my garden, which is designed on the old cottage garden principle of close planting so that there is hardly any room for weeds, I specialise in things I can cut for flower arranging the year around, for photography, show and exhibition work, or simply enjoying in the house.

In this book I would like to invite you into my home and to walk around the garden with me through the seasons. Clearly I cannot hope to list every flower, seedhead, and leaf available every month through the year. In any case, things will differ in various parts of the country and according to the weather. But just to whet the appetite, you will find after each month my list of some of the things you may find in the garden and in the shops.

I hope this book will bring you pleasure and perhaps fresh inspiration, whether you arrange flowers purely for relaxation at home or whether you fancy the exciting world of shows and exhibitions.

JANUARY

Yet just arrangement, rarely brought to pass
But by a master's hand, disposing well
The gay diversities of leaf and flow'r,
Must lend its aid t' illustrate all their charms,
And dress the regular yet various scene.

William Cowper

January, bringer of the year, sweeps in, a lusty, blustery month with the after-Christmas sales in full swing, snow in the wind, and the earth battened down under frost. A month when apples wither in the store, and sunroom and conservatory and closed-in porch welcome the indoor hyacinth, pale daffodil, and striped crocus.

We dream around the fire of the year to come, every smallest flower is a miracle, and a walk which yields a trail of scarlet blackberry leaves brings great happiness.

Personally, I always take the Christmas decorations down as soon as possible after New Year has set in – suddenly they look tawdry and over-hearty and I long for fresh flowers once again, with their light scents and foretaste of spring. Unfortunately this is the month when we have to think most carefully how to get the interest of fresh colour into our winter lives as the cold bites, the afternoons gloom up, and shop flowers are at their most expensive.

Buying cut flowers

The florists' shops in town are bright with lovely things – daffodils, tulips, orchids, freesias, and other forced hothouse beauties, so that at least once a month I am tempted in to buy a bunch of violets or anemones or the first narcissus, for being a gardener, I don't often buy myself cut flowers. The very business of stepping into a flower shop in winter is a delight.

I always choose buds or very newly-opened blooms as these will obviously last much longer than flowers which are already wide open, and I keep the arrangement as cool as possible, even removing it from a warm room at night, to give it the longest possible life. Don't be afraid to cut down the stalks, for stems of varying lengths make the arrangement more interesting.

It's worth remembering that:

★ Double flowers are more opulent-looking and always last longer than single-petalled blooms, so look out for double tulips, double daffodils, and double freesias.

★ Short-stemmed flowers sometimes cost less than long-stemmed.

★ Tulips last longer than daffodils.

★ A single perfect rose or a spray carnation with numbers of buds should last 9

longer than a bunch of mimosa or violets, so is a better buy.

★ Anemones, especially when just about to open bud, will last a very long time and when their petals have fallen will keep the fluffy purple boss of stamens to add interest to a new arrangement of fresh flowers.

★ Bulb flowers enjoy being arranged in quite shallow water, but often resent the water-retaining foams sold for flower arranging, being among the few flowers with this tendency.

★ Chincherinchees last for many weeks indoors if in bud when brought home. Be sure to cut off the waxed stem ends.

★ Chrysanthemums, particularly spray chrysanthemums, are extremely good stayers.

Out of doors

If you don't feel like buying cut flowers, there is no need to feel bored or deprived, for there is so much of interest to see and do in January. A walk, even alone, in the countryside is quite sure to bring many small joys as well as a tingling face – perhaps a nicely-shaped mossy stone, a small branch of interesting shape blown down in the last gale, an old bird's nest from a hedge, an empty snail shell striped like a humbug, and a couple of pheasant or pigeon feathers.

If you live near the sea, a family drive down to the beach on a mild day might be rewarding, particularly after a winter storm, to look for pieces of wave-sculptured driftwood, shells, old fishing floats, pebbles, bits of rock, and dried seaweed washed in on the tide. These will make bases or accessories for arrangements to come.

Fresh spring flowers and pot plants in the conservatory – outside there's snow.

Silk flowers from a wedding hat and dried larkspur in an antique chest.

10

Or what about spending a Saturday afternoon looking round the junk stalls of the local market or going around the January sales with an eye open for knock-down-price containers for flowers, or such oddments as fancy candles left over from Christmas? One of my own best January buys some years ago was two sprays of cut-price silk roses meant for decorating a hat, and I have been using them every winter since.

Catkins and pussy willows

Out along the country lanes and in the woods, swinging lambstail catkins and neat pussy willows are already forming. A stem or two will help make a few flowers go a long way, and after a week or so small welcome leaves should emerge. I take care not to gather too much, and I try not to damage the tree or bush at all.

When pussy willow is already in its chicken-yellow fluffiness it is already 'past it' so far as flower arrangers are concerned, for it will last only a day or two longer. Picked in bud, it has a long life expectancy and will eventually achieve the fluffy look, if you don't mind the pollen on your table top.

In the garden I have lots of catkins almost out. By the front door in the sunny shelter of the house the long silver-grey (and very expensive-looking) catkins of *Garrya elliptica* (the silk tassel bush) create a soft waterfall of colour against the blue-green wash of the wall. A few stems in a tall vase-shaped container make a homely arrangement, allowing the catkins to show off. I have found, by the way, that the catkins preserve easily, as do all the flowering hazels and willows if you leave them out of water in an arrangement for a week or two. They are, however, best of all properly preserved by giving them a shallow three-weeks' long drink of one part glycerine to two parts of hot water. After preserving, paint the base of each stem with nail varnish to prevent rot and you can arrange them with fresh flowers for years to come.

Jasmine

On most days, whatever the weather, I take at least one walk around my garden, under the jasmine arch where the bluetits feed and up the narrow stone path by the edge of the lawn, across the paved sitting-in-the-sun-in-the-summer area, and into the 'secret' garden where the hellebores grow, to see what new thing is out today.

Winter jasmine (*Jasminum nudiflorum*) is a real treasure in the bleak months and I am constantly surprised that there are still flower-lovers' gardens around which don't contain this winter treat. The starry golden flowers stud the slim bare sprays from November onwards and go on intermittently, depending on the weather, until about March. Grow it on a sheltered wall if you can, though I have it on each side of a terrace door facing north, as well as in a storm-tossed shower over an open archway opposite the same door. I like to have winter flowers where you can see them from the house. If frosts endanger the 11

expanding flowers I just cut a few of the frosted sprays and bring them indoors. Here fresh new stars are soon coaxed out by the warm room. After picking the flowers I always give them a short warm-water drink before arranging them. I specially like to place an arrangement of winter jasmine on a small table under a lamp, and I always try to include some of these bright, hopeful flowers in any bunch I may take to some housebound victim of a winter cold.

When I go up to London to have lunch, perhaps, with a magazine editor or a town-based friend I always carry with me a tiny nosegay which will include my own winter jasmine. I always see that gift flowers are given a good deep drink overnight. The following morning I arrange the winter posy in my hand, adding perhaps a frill of ivy or lemon geranium leaves, binding the stems together fairly firmly with darning wool and sheathing the whole thing in clear plastic self-seal kitchen wrap. The nostalgic old name tussie-mussie for these flowery mixtures is sadly not in fashion, but is a charming one. Into my tussie-mussies in January might go any number of appealing small things, such as primroses gathered from a sheltered spot, some sprigs of wintersweet (*Chimonanthus praecox*), laurustinus, and sprays of the semi-double winter prunus (*Prunus subhirtella autumnalis*).

This last winter pleasure for a cosy corner can flower on and off in mild spells for up to six of the autumn, winter, and spring months. I grow the pink form, though there is a white one, and in my last two gardens I have had it in the shelter of the front of the house. My own first delighted discovery of this prunus came after a long car journey with a friend one mild but foggy January day to a nursery in the New Forest, where she was to pick up an order. As we struck out from the car park to 'find the man' we suddenly saw through the mist this enchanting, delicate tree, its slim branches floating in a haze of palest pink flowers. I decided there and then to have it. We drove home through the darkening afternoon with one window of the car open to accommodate the bobbing top of my tree and the car was filled with a soft froth of colour as I held on to the great root-ball covered in sacking leaving the driver just about enough room to change gear!

Since that time the plant-in-container boom has come along and instant gardening with a tree in full flower is nothing unusual. Then, it was like something out of a fantasy.

Hellebores

Gardens can look just as good in winter as at any other time if we plant the right things. Dwarf and slow-growing conifers, with their variety of colours, come into their own both as a neat form of garden decoration and to provide cut plant material for indoor arrangements. Slow-growing conifers along with other evergreens make the setting of my own winter garden, but the chief colour, the jam on the cake, comes from flowers. Most people know about the Christmas rose (*Helleborus niger*) but fewer know the handsome Lenten rose (*Helleborus*

orientalis) with green-white flowers, or of some of the other gorgeous hellebores.

All the hellebores are perfectly hardy but they may suffer in any prolonged spell of frost, the flowers keeling over and sometimes never really recovering from the ordeal of it all. They can be grown in a garden frame, which shields them from the weather and ensures very early flowers. Or hellebores may be covered with cloches, and I have also seen Christmas roses growing successfully in a big tub in an open porch.

The Lenten hellebores come in a rich variation of colour, including pastel ribbon pinks, soft wine–dark purples, and ruby, as well as very refreshing greens, creams, and white. Some are attractively freckled, all are so desirable, as is even the unkindly-named 'stinking hellebore', *Helleborus foetidus*, a rare wild native plant which hangs its small jade-green winter bells in pendant clusters, each flower neatly tipped as it matures with an edging of maroon.

Helleborus corsicus produces great fountains of flowerheads, each bloom like a clear green Chinese porcelain bowl holding a pale green sea anemone. The leathery leaves, too, are quite invaluable for cutting, lasting exceptionally well in water. Real outdoor girls, these last two hellebores require no winter

Hellebore heads arranged on a plate which is covered with kitchen cling film will last a week with or without water. *Sprigs of parsley, and geranium leaves, set off the flowers. The clear green flower (centre) is* Helleborus corsicus.

13

protection, I find. In the summer no one notices them in my garden but in the winter . . . well, Cinderella comes into her own! Plant them, by the way, in full sun. Ignore writers who advise you to plant in shade!

Hellebores are notoriously difficult as cut flowers, particularly when gathered young. As with all cut flowers, pick and pop straight into water – carrying a jug or bucket round the garden with you. Hellebores must then have a shallow boiling-water drink before being arranged in plenty of water. I find it helpful, too, to slice open one side of the stem completely, from top to bottom with your thumbnail or the point of a nail file, to help them drink.

Individual heads preserve perfectly in any of the special flower drying mediums that can be bought, perhaps, at flower club sales tables. But one of my favourite ways with hellebores, not only because it is so economical of the flowers but because it makes them last a whole week, is again to take only odd, short-stemmed flowerheads and a few opening buds complete with a bit of green. Then, choosing a plain-coloured plate to go with the blooms, I arrange them as nicely as I can all over it (there is no need for water). Then I cover the plate with a piece of clear kitchen plastic taken smoothly over the flowers and round to the back of the plate. I carry hellebores this way to show when I lecture

There is always something available for a quick decoration. Here colour comes to a corner of the kitchen with baskets of lentils, red beans and other pulses.

about my garden at this time of year, passing the flower-bedecked plate around the audience. Incidentally, this is also an interesting way to display single-petalled anemone flowerheads.

Flower arrangers develop a 'seeing eye' for the beauty which surrounds them where others might pass it by. Forced rhubarb tops, for example, are lime-green and often have a pinky streak – beautiful at any time but invaluable in the winter, when they can be arranged with anemones or daffodils or simply on their own. Lentils, peppercorns, split green peas, red beans are all natural plant forms and are among the everyday colourful things which can be pressed into use. Fill a shallow brown cooking dish with lentils, for example, and bury a pinholder near the centre back to hold two or three stout stems of last year's Queen Anne's Lace seedheads, and you will see the sort of thing I mean. I have baskets of pulses around the kitchen for their colour.

There's a lot to be said for having a little sunroom conservatory. Ours is lovely this month – cosy and welcoming, and I try to keep it looking colourful when seen from the lane. Moreover, when the French doors leading out of the sitting room are opened, a soft waft of Roman hyacinth, daffodil, and freesia perfume flows into the house.

The indoor bulb flowers are at their best now. I never buy the specially prepared bulbs for forcing into flower by Christmas, nor do I plant my indoor bulbs too early. There is plenty of colour around the house at Christmas, so I like to have bulbs in dishes and bowls coming into bloom when Twelfth Night has whisked away the festive decorations.

Houseplants

Flowering houseplants, like those received as Christmas presents, or the ones we buy for ourselves this month, given proper after-flowering care, can be re-introduced to the house next year in full bloom again. With a new plant, ensure that it is well wrapped when you bring it out of the shop – some shop assistants carefully wrap up the pot but leave the wrapping wide open at the top.

There is much mystique about pot plants, but the main problems usually boil down to over-hot rooms and nervous watering. In fact, watering is the worst headache. After many years of enthusiastically growing indoor plants of every description I pass on my tip for all those grown in pots with a drainage hole in the bottom: when they need a drink, take them to the kitchen and submerge the whole of the pot in a bowl of water which has had the chill taken off. See how the bubbles rise; they mean that the air in the pot is being forced out and replaced by water. Splash just a little water over the plant, and when the pot has stopped gurgling take it out and leave it to drain really well before returning it to its usual place.

You can add a few drops of one of the proprietary plant-feeds to the water; I save any such water and use it to water plants in pots with no drainage holes. As with the majority of indoor plants, the time to water is only when the soil seems 15

A foliage plant in a big rosy jug from a junk stall wins extra colour on a winter day, with matching sprays of artificial fuchsias made of silk. Instant interest!

Silhouetted against a snowy landscape, shop-bought daffodils teamed with sprays of shrubby honeysuckle from the garden, on a pinholder in a modern container.

dry to the touch, or when a normally perky plant suddenly begins to droop its flowers or leaves.

I have found the following ideas helpful with certain house plants.

Indoor azalea: To begin with, never allow your azalea to dry out completely. Keep it as cool as you can. Set the pot on a saucer containing a few pebbles, which are kept moist. In 'hard' water areas use only rain water. Regularly spray the plant with a fine mist sprayer; this will keep it happy and help prevent attack by red spider. In summer, the plant can go outdoors in a shady spot, its pot buried in a border.

Cineraria: These handsome plants, with their clear singing look-at-me colours of pink, red, white, blue, or purple clusters of daisy-like flowers, enjoy a cool, light situation such as a sunless window ledge. If a cineraria, or indeed any houseplant, gets an attack of greenfly or whitefly, a proprietary spray will make a quick killing, though you may have to repeat the treatment.

African violet (Saintpaulia): I grow these on a steamy kitchen window ledge and have never found them the notoriously difficult subjects they are often said to be. Watering from below, and standing the pot on moist pebbles, is helpful. Try not to wet the leaves. Pull off old foliage right down to the base. An

16 interesting way to propagate is to take a leaf complete with a bit of stem and

stand it in a glassful of water or plant it in one of the special houseplant rooting bags now available, placed in the kitchen window.

Christmas cactus (Zygocactus): Many of us will know of an ancient example of one of these striking plants, with their crab-like foliage and Madame Butterfly flowers resembling shocking pink, red, or apricot double fuchsias. Water the plants very stingily. I keep mine rather dry, in the sunny porch, throughout the summer and only begin to water them frequently when I bring them indoors about October. This treatment seems to 'ripen' the plant, although it is important that it should always be watered just sufficiently to keep the foliage nice and plump-looking.

When brought into the house, the leaf-ends soon begin to sprout promisingly with pendulous buds, and they are always in flower for Christmas. A Christmas cactus grown as an indoor winter hanging basket plant will trail nicely. These plants, incidentally, are said to drop their buds if you turn the pot round but this is just not so; I find that by regular turning, over the years, new growth is made all round and the flowers cascade attractively over the pot at every side.

Poinsettia: You either love or hate these plants! As well as the fiery dragon reds there are pink and cream-white kinds. The 'petals' are really long-lived bracts; the real flowers are the smaller yellow bits in the centre. Poinsettias like a light spot, but not direct sunlight, and must be freely watered and kept warm; always use water with the chill taken off it. They are difficult to bring back to their original colourful glory for a second year, but a well-grown plant is handsome in its own right for its beautiful green foliage.

An old window keeps the frost off early hellebores blooming outdoors in January.
When flowers are scarce, any well-grown houseplant can spare a bloom and leaf or two.

17

Cyclamen: I sometimes pull off the odd flower or two for an arrangement. Never cut a stem, leaving a piece behind to rot the crown. Give a weekly feed, and when the plant *really* needs a drink put it in a bowl of water and afterwards drain well. I have successfully brought the same plants into flower for two or three years. They like light, airy conditions not excessively hot. After flowering finishes, leave the plant on its side in a shady place and let it completely dry out.

Heathers: Never allow the compost to dry right out, but when the plants go out of flower they have to be discarded, for heathers in pots are a purely temporary pleasure.

Winter-flowering begonias: These are an excellent buy, and many types and colours have been developed. They like the warmth of central heating, but keep them out of draughts and remove all dead flowers for continuity of bloom.

Chrysanthemums: Treat them as temporary pot plants, and either discard them after flowering or plant them in the garden.

Christmas cherry (*Solanum capsicastrum*): This cheerful fellow with its green-ripening-to-orange fruits sometimes disappoints by shedding leaves and fruits, usually if it has been allowed to dry out or is in a poor light. It likes regular feeding and a sunny window.

Primulas: *P. malacoides* (the fairy primulas) are usually not expensive to buy, and make very good, long-lasting houseplants. Along with *P. sinensis* and *P. obconica*, they seem to enjoy life all the more if they can be kept in cool conditions. My sister specialises in making a big feature of them in her just-frost-free porch, planting them in pretty pots. Despite their reputation for disliking draughts we both find that when well grown they don't care two hoots about the constant opening and closing of doors, indeed they seem to thrive on it. Keep an eye on watering and never allow the root ball to dry right out and the plants will flower away for you month after month.

Containers for indoor plants

Speaking of pretty pots – to a flower arranger any item which is used for holding cut flowers is called a container; it might be anything from expensive hand-made modern pottery to Granny's old cream jug. Few arrangers, I find, think of using their collection of containers to display potted plants, but personally, I dislike seeing my lovely plants ranged in dreary ranks along the window ledges in plastic pots. They look so much more comfortable and at home when either planted alone or in companionable groups in something more decorative taken from the flower arrangement shelves. Specially useful to me are large bowls, urns and vegetable dishes and baskets with liners. I even use my wrought-iron 'church' flower pedestal, as its bowl displays trailing subjects well.

Even waste-paper bins are pressed into service in my house: a black japanned one with an oriental garden design is striking for indoor palms. A cheap brown plastic office waste-bin sets off forced daffodils and ferns, and later in the year, foliage geraniums.

Plants of every kind will do well in containers without drainage holes if you are careful about not over-watering. You either put the potted plant straight into the chosen outer container, or you can plant several items together in compost in the more decorative object: short plants and trailers to the front, taller, more upright, further back. As in flower arrangement, contrast the

An asymmetrical triangle arrangement of double and single tulips plus eucalyp- *tus foliage. Double flowers and those in bud last longest as cut flowers.*

shapes and colours and textures and I'm sure you'll be very pleased. In January I like to add a few bulbs from the garden just coming into bloom and I dig up oddments such as nicely budding primroses to add to the effect.

Flowers and plants together

Cut flowers, too, can be included in this kind of arrangement of indoor plants; to hold the water, use for example, such things as small hidden fish paste jars. Try bunches of violets with potted pink cyclamen, yellow polyanthus with green-and-white striped chlorophytum, for instance. If real flowers are unavailable, or simply too expensive this month, you might like to add a silk flower or two. I have quite a collection of these and among my best 'cheats' this January are orange tiger lilies which are blossoming happily away in the dining room on a tall overwintering geranium. In here they match up well with the warm coral of the velvet seat covers.

Also effective are scarlet and green mock fruits which I have cunningly set among the leaves of an overwintering plumbago at the far end of the conservatory. This last has temporarily puzzled even a keen visiting botanist – which pleased me enormously. I commend to you such small deceptions this month, but the trick, the amusement, begins to wear thin as the plants move into spring, so then I pack my gay deceivers away for another year.

Like many other families we have a closed-in unheated glass porch with a door at the front of the house. Ours happens to face south, which is nice, and it is a great happiness to me every month of the year. In winter it is a special challenge to keep it looking bright and welcoming with flowers.

I love it particularly at night, when the lamps in the porch are lit and the flowering plants behind the glass look rich and extravagant from the lane. But in fact the majority are hardy plants, like coloured primroses and polyanthus, and ferns lifted from the open garden and planted in long white troughs which fit the shelves. I have a succession of troughs coming along planted up to give perfume and colour. They include hyacinth and pansy, lavender and white drumstick primula, crocus and *Iris danfordiae* (a stout small iris of bright lemon yellow) and later on there will be short double pink and white tulips.

Geraniums (pelargoniums) surprisingly come through most winters out here in the airy porch. I continue watering them in mild spells and give them the very occasional feed so that they stay in flower. This is a good place, too, for potted houseplant azaleas and cyclamen; I find they go on flowering for months in the cooler air. January can treat us peevishly, and it is very satisfying to use flowers and plants to cheer up not only ourselves but also anyone who calls.

Flowers in January

From the garden: Christmas roses, jasmine, winter-flowering heathers.
From the shops: Daffodils, 'Paper White' narcissi, gladioli, chrysanthemums,
roses, carnations, freesias, and decorative fruits and vegetables.

FEBRUARY

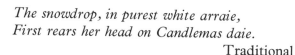

The snowdrop, in purest white arraie,
First rears her head on Candlemas daie.

Traditional

F ebruary fill-dyke, and all that. Think of February, and you think of rain weeping down the window panes and thin, iced, knockabout winds pursuing everything, and turning the puppies' ears inside-out. Foxes call at night. Occasional light snow puts all but the bravest off gardening.

Yet this is also the hopeful month, dedicated to St Valentine and fresh small excitements like new-born lambs and the robin starting to sing.

Snowdrops

Snowdrops, or *Galanthus nivalis* to give them their upstage name (under which you will find them in the glossy bulb catalogues), are February's own speciality. The name snowdrop, by the way, is not derived from a drop of snow but from the snow-white Elizabethan pearl ear-drop, which is a pretty thought. You're said by tradition to be able to pick your first one on old Candlemas Day, February 2, and astonishingly I am always able to find the first few in bloom, nestled in some protected spot, perhaps at the foot of the house wall, on that day no matter what the weather. I make a point of picking a small bunch.

Candlemas Bells, Fair Maids of February . . . the snowdrop has plenty of old country names. It is among many flowers dedicated to Mary the mother of Jesus as her special emblem, and it is interesting that this once wild native flower, so associated with country gardens, was grown by the early monks in monastic orchards and gardens.

The snowdrop bulbs which are sold in their thousands every year for pots and gardens can be disappointing and not come through. The snowdrop is best planted 'in the green', which means still in full leaf just after flowering. A few firms sell them like this, but if you have a friend who will give you a clump to start you off you will find that they soon spread and can make good groups. Always plant them in clumps as they look best clustered close and not spaced apart. I usually find my first snowdrops come out in a south-facing border, which is a really good place to plant them.

As our garden slopes gently upwards from the white wicket gate in the lane to the highest point in the orchard, so the snowdrops planted at various points vary in their opening times and we can enjoy them for some weeks. Those under

the fruit trees sometimes do not push through until mid-March, and this nicely extends the picking season. I like to arrange them indoors in small containers standing on a bit of mirror glass to reflect their delicate pale green inner markings. In the midlands and north their time of blooming is I think usually later than in the south.

Shrubs

There are so many super flowers out this month in my garden. For instance, laurustinus (*Viburnum tinus*). This evergreen shrub is so easy to grow, and produces masses of flowers (followed by berries), right the way through the winter and often in autumn and spring too. The clustered blooms open from pink buds. *V. tinus* 'Eve Price' is even more attractive, with its deeper pink buds and pale pink flowers. You can pick them in all weathers.

I like to mass laurustinus blooms, cut on short stems, in a low round bowl, and they look sweet and smell nice in a treasured Victorian glass cornucopia, or on shorter stems in the lustreware cup and saucer which have survived from my granny's first tea service. The flowers of any hard-stemmed shrubs last longer if you scrape the bark off the part of the stem which will be under water, and also make a slit down the stem at the bottom to enable more water to be taken in.

With all cut plants, any leaves which might go below water level should be taken off (you can do this in the garden as you gather them). Removing these leaves prevents them decaying and clouding the water, and avoids the necessity to keep changing it. Top up the water level as the flowers and leaves drink it up. During the first few hours after the arrangement has been completed the plant material takes up a considerable amount of water, and it is worth checking so that you can top up as soon as necessary. Leaves will usually stay fresh far longer than flowers and can be left *in situ* while new flowers are added.

Three chrysanthemum sprays cheer a winter day. A homely design.

A Victorian glass cornucopia arranged with short-stemmed sweet peas.

Early flowers for cutting

There are many early flowers which do, perhaps surprisingly, cut well and last well. These include winter-flowering crocus, such as *Crocus chrysanthus* 'Snow Bunting', finely patterned like the wings of the bird after which it is named, with rich dark lilac feathering on cream; 'Advance', soft golden yellow with dark maroon streaking and feathering on the outside of its outer petals; quick-spreading 'Tommies', *C. tomasinianus*, which come in pale lavender and deeper colours; and indeed a number of others with petals like fine porcelain, which really do flower some time before their larger spring-flowering cousins.

I often pick a few crocus for indoors, and they mistake the warmth for the sun and quickly open, so that their attractive centres show up. They look well arranged quite alone, simply clustered together with a few leaves in an eggcup or a doll's house size bowl. Winter crocus should really be better known, for they provide such cheer on these cold blustery February days.

Aconites

Winter aconites, with their pert Dog Toby ruffs of green setting off the golden flowers, are also early on the scene. I remember seeing them some years ago as a result of a report in our local newspaper. It told how a titled lady who lives just outside the town had invited the members of a local organisation to supper and afterwards had escorted them round the moonlit garden to see the aconites which, said the report, were a marvellous sight, swarming across a hillside in their thousands. She opened the garden to the public a little later, and it was something I could not miss. Parking the car, we walked smartly down the long drive, past the house, and along a number of paths, all the way directed by hand-written notices on sticks saying 'Aconites this way', 'Follow arrows to aconites', or simply 'Aconites'. Appetites could not have been better whetted. And there, suddenly, they were – a whole hillside of them on the other side of low park railings, a unique sight.

Lonicera

Everyone who has a garden, no matter how small, can have winter flowers. Why is the delectable winter honeysuckle so little known? *Lonicera fragrantissima*, its proper name, is very descriptive. The fragile-looking white flowers are set off by quiet brown stems. The shrub is best planted near a south wall or under the light cover of a tree so that the frost does not brown the sweet-scented blossoms as they appear.

Forcing into early flower

In winter, when plant material is scarce, arranging can be even more interesting (as things which have to be worked for generally are). Coaxing a few stems to break into premature leaf or flower is an integral part of the winter scene for a keen flower arranger, and February is a very good time to start. Most people 23

grow forsythia and flowering currant (ribes). These, along with prunus, horse chestnut, hawthorn, and so on, already have fat buds beginning to form. Bring a few nicely-shaped pieces indoors. Either put them into a jug of hot water and leave them in a warmish place to come out, or else arrange them at once, using very warm water in the container. After a few weeks they will open into pale green leaf or flower.

Some will force in a dark place. I find that a toothpaste-pink flowering currant and a carnation-pink prunus in my garden both open bridal-white indoors when forced out early in this way. Such stems will sell easily, making them good money-spinners for flower club sales tables, charity markets, and the like, for few can resist out-of-season flowers. Among other branches to force into early flower or leaf when their buds plump up are willow, pear, apple, plum, lilac, magnolia, hazel, and japonica (*Chaenomeles*).

For a quick flower arrangement, choose at least one piece of budding branch which looks something like a small curving tree. Place a pinholder in a shallow cooking dish, slightly off-centre and towards the back, and impale the 'tree' on it. You will find that, no matter how curvy the stem, if you position it so that the tip comes immediately above the foot (where it meets the pinholder) it will look nicely balanced. One or two shorter budding twigs can be added, or a few flowers or leaves with the stems cut to different lengths, to spring closely from the foot of the 'tree'. Now add a bit of mossy wood, a few suitably sized stones, or perhaps a small pottery figurine to add interest for the eye and to hide the pinholder. The twiggy outline of the design will stand in a stylish way until the flowers open on the 'tree', and the additional flowers and leaves can be replaced as required.

Equipment

To begin arranging flowers need cost little. Many necessary items will already be in the house. You will need:

★ As many containers as possible, and half the fun of the hobby is collecting these. They may include, apart from 'proper' containers, such things as deep ashtrays, china and metal candlesticks, ceramic or wooden boxes, pillboxes, plastic plant pot saucers, pottery cooking dishes, and all kinds of similar homely items.

★ Chicken wire – cheap, soft, two-inch (50 mm) mesh which crumples easily and is used for holding stems in place inside containers.

★ Pinholders, including at least one well pinholder and a candlecup.

★ A pair of really sharp kitchen scissors, special florists' scissors, snips or secateurs.

★ A deep bucket, for pre-arrangement drinks for flowers and leaves.

★ A block of water-retaining foam, sold under various trade names. Soak it for ten minutes in a bowl of hot water before arranging flowers and leaves in it,

and do not allow it to dry out when in use.

*A stem of spray carnations, which
should last a fortnight, is worth buying.*

★ Rubber bands to hold foam or chicken wire firmly in containers, or narrow transparent sticky tape to criss-cross over the foam or wire and under the container.
★ Toothpicks for pressing into fruits and the stems of some bulb flowers to hold them on pinholders etc.
★ Dry foam for use when making arrangements of dried plant material.
★ An atomiser to spray arrangements and keep them fresh.
★ A proprietary spray such as 'Leafshine', if you like to see glossy leaves in an arrangement.

Arrangements with fruit

Creating an arrangement with everyday fruits at this time of year is every bit as colourful and appealing to the eye as using expensive flowers if you have nothing to gather in the garden. Just display the things you have around the house waiting to be eaten. Think of it – all those warm red glossy apples, tomatoes, pale green matt-textured pears, cheerful yellow lemons, perfumed tangerines and oranges, a bunch of grapes perhaps, even a peach, or maybe two, some nuts and a few scrubbed vegetables. What colours, shapes and textures they all have! Arrange them extravagantly, positioning a strong colour here for a highlight, oval shapes against round, and so on. Arrange them dramatically in a container with a stem, or in a shallow wicker basket, on a piece of mirror glass, a plain pottery plate or a wooden bread board. Each will create a different effect. One or two small jars or bottles hidden among the fruits can hold water for, say, 25

a few bold leaves, a cluster of daffodils or tulips, a knot of anemones. A wine bottle added to the group might make a sort of still-life picture.

In Victorian times fruit was often arranged as a static decoration in complex pyramids with flowers for dinner tables. Edwardian ladies too liked to have fruit as the table decoration right through the meal. Sometimes leaves of Virginia creeper, vine, berberis, ivy or laurel were placed singly among the fruits as a contrast, while simple fruit pyramids were used to decorate even the breakfast table. But cut flowers among the fruits were certainly not approved of in earlier days as I found when I came upon a fascinating quotation from a diary written in 1670. It told of a dinner with the Marquis of Worcester, Lord Stafford, and the Lieutenant of the Tower of London present, and said that when the dessert of fruit was set upon the table 'Lord Stafford rose in some disorder because there were roses stuck about the fruits. Such an antipathie it seems he had to them as Lady Selinger also had'. Apparently the dear lady had once been pricked by a rose thorn! The story is interesting because it shows how even then flowers, and fruit meant to be eaten, were arranged together.

Glass containers

Mention of the Victorians and Edwardians reminds me of how much they liked every sort of glass container for flowers, leaves and sometimes fruits. Glass, now so out of favour for flowers, was the 'in' thing for many years until shortly after the last war, when, oddly I think, people began to object to the sight of the stems showing through the water. And so silver plated epergnes (often with ruby, clear and cut glass trumpet-shaped flower holders), the prettiest little pressed-glass flower baskets, opaline vases, violet glasses (meant to take a fat shop bunch of big heavily scented Parma violets complete with a frill of leaves) and cut glass rose-bowls with silver mesh tops were all sent packing to the jumble sales.

Now, I believe, glass is just about due for a comeback. Certainly much coloured glass is very decorative and there is great appeal in the sparkling well-designed container of coloured glass set to stand where it catches the light from a window or a lamp after dark, with slim green stems gleaming through.

For some years I have been quietly collecting glass flower containers when I have seen them, picking them up from junk stalls and sometimes flower club sales tables. The more beautiful and delicate Victorian and Edwardian glass is now becoming an expensive antique shop find and the last epergne I saw was priced at well over £100 by the shop man, who said 'they're all being shipped to America' – so I still don't have an epergne. However, most of us have a number of glass things about the house which could be used for holding a few cut flowers.

When flowers were first cut and put into water it is certain that they were arranged in homely, everyday containers meant to hold other things. We might take a tip from our forebears and place a few winter garden snippings, an early primrose or two, a jasmine sprig, or a bit of winter honeysuckle, in any nicely-shaped and suitably sized clear or coloured glass object from the kitchen

*Pots of hyacinth, polyanthus and fern
planted up in an authentic Constance
Spry container with a few cut sprays of
winter-flowering laurustinus.*

cupboard, and simply enjoy the flowers for themselves.

Empty wine bottles of dark nut-brown or soft moss-green glass make stable containers for a spray or two of early leaves and flowers, with the stems slipped directly into the neck of the bottle. For a more elaborate arrangement using a bottle or decanter as if it were a stemmed container, a gadget called a candlecup, which holds either a piece of water-retaining foam or a pinholder and crumpled-up chicken wire, is invaluable. (A candlecup is a shallow bowl with a short stem which can be pushed into bottles or candlesticks.)

For show work, see-through glass is not usually suitable. It disturbs the design, tending to shine and catch the eye over-much, so that the container becomes more important than the plant material (and in competitive work the plant material must always be the dominant factor). A contrary fault is that, particularly in a show niche, glass has a way of seeming to disappear from view if the light is not just right, giving the odd effect of the flowers floating in space instead of the container acting as a link between flowers and table top or base.

Glass is a good choice at home for showing off the delicate flower shapes and colours of springtime and early summer. It is not usually so harmonious with bolder, heavier flowers and leaves. Cleaning quite intricate glass pieces is easy if you use one of the special tablets or powders available in packs.

Colour matching

Whenever I buy flowers or plants I try to make a special point of choosing colours to go with a room . . . perhaps to link up with its cushion covers, tone with curtains, or contrast with the carpet. My sitting room has white walls, plain rose-pink carpet and, here and there in the furnishings, touches of carnation and cyclamen-pink, pale lilac, kingfisher blue, and softest apple green. Tints and tones of all these colours can be used successfully in flower arrangements in the room, and it is a never-ending interest and enjoyment to play up and dramatise first one colour then another, according to whatever cut blooms or flowering pot plants I happen to have.

At this time, one of my jobs is tidying up the early forced-bulb flowers, taking off the last blooms for arranging. I keep the bulbs watered until the foliage dies down; they are then planted out in the garden. Sweet peas can be started into growth this month, and overwintering geraniums watered and fed regularly as they begin to sprout into growth again. And so we are through cold, bleak February in quick sticks, and ready for March to come striding in . . .

Flowers in February

From the garden: Mahonia flowers and leaves, Iris stylosa (unguicularis), snowdrops, *Cornus mas*, *Iris reticulata*, crocus, aconites, *Viburnum fragrans*, primroses, dicentra, stock and bulb flowers forced in the sunroom.

From the shops: Chain stores have early polyanthus in pots. Florists have violets, anemones, mimosa, carnations and possibly lily-of-the-valley.

MARCH

I leave this notice on my door
For each accustom'd visitor:
'I am gone into the fields
To take what this sweet hour yields'.
                    Percy Bysshe Shelley

The winds of March would be really quite jolly if they were not still so keen and cool. Whirls of last year's dead oak leaves, like cornflakes crisp from the packet, collect together on the newly turned flower beds and borders, and emerging crocus and daffodils appear with lop-sided collars or hats of dry brown leaves. Birds sing early and late, and get on with nest building. There are both wild and garden daffodils out, and the first hikers are plodding up the lane. Fields and gardens seem raked clean, the sun comes out, and the air is filled with a sense of unrest.

You can't actually declare it is spring, they say, until you can put your foot on six meadow daisies all at once. You could easily do it in my lane this month, because, by the garden gate and edging the stone step, I planted a row of small pink double 'Dresden China' daisies years ago, and despite having to put up with awful growing conditions, tramping feet, and the gravelly soil, they are always early into flower.

Market stalls are a good source of supply for daisies and all sorts of boxed plants. There will be primroses and polyanthus in a tempting colour range; aubrietia, purple, pink and red; yellow alyssum; pansies of all colours; white iberis. With such plants it is easy to give any home a fresh country look this month. Plant yellow and white primroses and a pansy or two into pots and perhaps put the pots into an old basket painted white to stand in the porch, on a window ledge or a balcony. Plant pots can be painted matt white, and the inside of the porch too, for an extra bit of dash and sparkle.

Posies

With luck a sudden swirl of sunny days will bring along the daffodils. And when I see daffodils I think of the lady who makes the delightful posies of flowers known as 'nosegays' which the Queen and other members of the Royal Family carry at the ceremony of the Royal Maundy on the day before Good Friday. At her garden gate, a little way from my home, hangs a sign 'By appointment to Her Majesty the Queen, suppliers of nosegays'. I must have passed the gate hundreds of times before I actually met the holder of the Royal Warrant, Mrs Valerie Bennett-Levy. The Maundy ceremony is held at a different cathedral or similar place of worship each year; Mrs Bennett-Levy told me how she sits up 29

all night with her daughter, two sons, and daughter-in-law making up the nosegays to ensure that they are absolutely fresh.

They are made in exactly the same way every year, and each deliciously scented. One in its paper ruff contains nine daffodils, fifteen narcissi, eleven stocks, fourteen violets, twelve primroses, twenty pieces of cupressus, eight sprigs of thyme, and ten stems of rosemary – ninety-nine items for each of the ten large nosegays. Four smaller ones are made for the children of the Royal Almonry. Many of the flowers and herbs which go into the nosegays come from the village gardens, the primroses from Devon. 'Every one of the Royal Family, especially Prince Philip, seems to enjoy the bunches,' the maker told me. 'They invariably bend their heads to take a sniff.'

You can make a spring arrangement of garden flowers, like a Victorian nosegay, by bunching your posy in one hand as you pick. Begin with one special flower in the centre and go on adding flowers in concentric rings finally adding a frill of leaves. Finish by binding the stems firmly with wool or fine wire, then slip the posy through a paper doyley with a cross cut in the centre, or use a special florists' frill. A small glass container will display such an arrangement with charm. It is generally believed that traditionally a rosebud should always be at the centre, but this is not so. According to *The Gardener*, in June, 1870, you could buy posies ready made at Covent Garden market and a favourite style was to have 'a white camellia at the centre, followed by a ring of roses, alternated with bunches of gentian, or blue cineraria, then a ring of scarlet geranium alternated with white stephanotis or deutzia. Here and there, in season, moss rose buds, heaths, lily of the valley sticking above the surface of the bouquet. Adiantum fern being a favourite green frill though common hard fern is used to fringe the commoner sorts. But the chief feature is the system of order in their arrangement.'

Using ornaments

During the early part of the month flowers are still hard to come by and in the shops, expensive. But every home has some small decorative object or ornament that can be worked into a flower decoration. It might be a Staffordshire pottery figure handed down in the family, or a seaside souvenir, some seashells, even an attractive plate or a book. Almost anything decorative and visually interesting can be used, and putting something like this in conjunction with a flower arrangement makes people look at familiar objects in a new way. Remember, though, that if you use an accessory in a competitive arrangement at a show the accessory must not dominate the plant material.

Try experimenting by placing an accessory in association with a few flowers. A well-chosen figurine, for example, can give a feeling of life and movement to a design; it can add extra colour and impact – a feeling of completing the picture. It can even tell a little story. Try placing it so that the eye is led easily from flowers to accessory and back again, giving an overall sense of harmony and

30

continuity. A position slightly off-centre, or to one side, is often a good one, and as the human face always draws the eye it is a good tip to turn a figurine slightly so that it appears to look back at the arrangement instead of staring you straight in the eye!

Similar ideas can become elegant decorations for the dining table. A favourite accessory of mine is a pink and white porcelain figure of a gardener leaning on his spade. This very old and delicate fellow normally spends his time on our sitting-room mantelpiece, but just once or twice a year I 'arrange' him with suitable small flowers, such as forget-me-nots, the sweet scented winter-flowering honeysuckle (*Lonicera fragrantissima*) I mentioned, sprays of the very small double pink prunus (*P. triloba*) or the pink 'lane' daisies and, later in the year, miniature roses. Why use this little figure so rarely? Because flowers and leaves must always be in good proportion to any chosen figurine, and anything even the size of a pansy or a crocus would be too big and overwhelming for so tiny a gardener.

That spring feeling! The design repeats the lively movement of the Twenties figurine. Sprays of forsythia sketch the line. Mixed leaves add impact.

Arrangement of leopard's bane (doro-nicum) with the golden-leaf form of mock orange. Doronicums are no use for shows as the flowers move to the light.

A base of some kind, incidentally, can often be useful for marrying the container, accessories, and plant material happily together, though at home the shelf or table on which they are grouped can sometimes act as the base. I often use a piece of old roofing slate which is kept outdoors so that it hangs on to its delicate lichen, an old bread board with the scrubbed worn patina of age, even pieces of floorboard whose edges have been softened by sanding with a home sanding machine.

Garden urns can be brought indoors, and flowers do not necessarily have to be arranged in them; they look more eye-catching sometimes with flowers and leaves arranged round them in the romantic eighteenth-century way seen in paintings of the period. I have a stone garden figurine of a girl holding a basket and she, brought indoors with care, makes a fine accessory to large party flowers and even sets off handsomely a grouping of pot plants. As there are already houseleeks growing in her basket, I find that some trails of these arranged at her feet make a good link.

32

Improving the view

Truly, few people could have a duller outlook than mine from the kitchen window! The kitchen window faces directly on to the high close-boarded boundary fence, plus a bit of next door's garage roof and a section of their kitchen wall. There is no room to plant a coloured shrub or a bit of creeper, and I reflect that in houses built nowadays the kitchen sink is usually nicely arranged to face the garden.

But I believe most things can be turned to advantage. My first thought was window boxes but, no, the window opens outwards. I edged the window with curtains (which I don't draw) that have a light-hearted design of flowers and birds, and fitted a striped pull-down blind which leaves room on the window ledge for a constantly changing panorama of flowers and plants and bits of colourful pottery. If I could have them in no other room I would concentrate flowers here, and I never weary of my 'view'. The secret is to ensure plenty of variety – for instance, I stand the plant pots in pottery mugs or containers coloured to look well with the curtains. Once I painted a number of ordinary plastic plant pots in traditional canal barge colours. The first step is to rub over the plastic pot with a piece of sandpaper and, after wiping it with a dry cloth, paint with gloss paint in dark green, navy blue, or donkey brown. When this is dry, paint over it your design of bold cabbage roses, daisies, or whatever, in pink, black, brilliant yellow, or pale leaf-green enamel. You might like to decorate your houseplant watering can to match. Empty fruit juice or baked bean tins could be painted similarly and used as plant containers.

Flowers for Mothering Sunday

> *Those who go a-mothering*
> *Find violets down the lane*

Mothering Sunday is the Sunday in mid-Lent when young people 'in service' at the big houses of the time, and working away from home, were allowed the day off to see their families. It was customary for them to take a simnel or mothering cake and a few fresh flowers. Violets and primroses and pussy willow picked in the country lanes, or something more choice like items begged from the gardener, were carried home to give with love.

Nowadays it is more usually shop flowers and plants which are presented to our mothers, but it has always been the thought that counts. Instead of commercially grown cut flowers, a garden pansy or a violet in full bloom in a pretty pot, with a ribbon bow, or a polyanthus just bursting into flower, looks just as attractive. It is important to think ahead and pot up some suitable plants a week or so before the big day, protecting them from the birds and the cold under a cloche, in the porch, or somewhere similarly sheltered so that they have at least three or four flowers out by the time they are needed.

Two little soft green ferns in the bowl of a big brandy glass, with a growing primrose, a purple crocus, and a few cotton wadding Easter chicks, make **33**

another pleasing and unusual gift. I always buy any small inexpensive containers I come across, keeping them for gift flowers.

For an arrangement of cut garden flowers to give away, any small bowl or tiny basket is ideal. Fill the bowl lightly with a bit of moss and simply press the flowers into it to hold the stems – primroses, early forget-me-nots, a sprig of wallflower, a spray or two of mahonia, an early pansy, whatever you happen to have. Give both flowers and leaves a good overnight drink and arrange them fresh just before you set off, adding water when you arrive.

Tiny baskets with a bowl inside, finished off with a bit of frivolous pale green

Potted plants together in an old veget-
able tureen, tallest at the back and
cascading forms over the sides and front
– a very attractive arrangement.

34

or lemon yellow ribbon, make a lovely gift for a child to take to Granny. Like most arrangements it will travel well even by car if loosely wrapped in a big plastic bag which covers everything. But for a really meticulously arranged job, the cut stems must go into chicken wire or Oasis, though you should bear in mind that most bulb flowers are not so happy arranged into the latter.

Flowers for cutting grown from seed
Here are some of my suggestions for good subjects to grow from seed for cutting:

Amaranthus: This is the catalogue name for the slim green chenille tassels of love-lies-bleeding (there is a red one). Sow the seed this month in a sunroom or warm greenhouse.

Atriplex: This beetroot-red beauty is something like a particularly handsome wild dock in its seedy state. Quite invaluable for cutting, but leave one of the plants to seed itself on for another year.

Calendula (marigold): Cheap and cheerful chaps in all the sunny colours (leave some seedheads on at the end of summer). Though the flowers may get smaller in subsequent years the seedling flowers are still charming. By the way, I always overwinter a pot of summer flowered marigolds in the porch where they continue on in bloom all winter and nicely into spring. The African and French marigolds are winners, too, with many new varieties now available.

Clarkia: An easily grown hardy annual with showy flowers. Sow outdoors in spring. Pretty colours make this a most useful thing to have around for flower arranging.

Didiscus caerulea: The light lavender-blue lace flowers of this half-hardy annual provide the most pleasing of cut flowers. Makes a fine indoor pot plant for the whole of the summer, or can be planted out in a warm sheltered place in the garden.

Euphorbia marginata (Snow on the Mountains): Useful for its showy green and white bracts.

Godetia: Very useful annuals for arranging; the flowers, like those of clarkia, will dry well for use in winter posies, using one of the special drying agents available.

Larkspur: Comes in pink, lavender, and white. Allow the blooms to open the full length of the stem. Pick and dry them for winter use.

Nasturtium: A packet of 'Alaska Mixed' is always a good buy, for the trails of cream marbled leaves are as cuttable as the flame, gold, and orange flowers.

Nicotiana (tobacco plant): *N. alata* gives us lime-green flowers which blend happily with most other colours in arrangements, but all make lovely summer flowers for decorating the garden.

Stocks: Well worth growing. Do try the Brompton stock for a long period of scented blossom. In sheltered sunny borders some flower all the winter and on into the spring.

35

Sweet peas: These are, I suppose, most people's favourites for cutting. Try the 'Antique Fantasy Mixed' for something really out of the ordinary. Very heavily scented, and in soft smudgy colours which might have been created especially to please flower arrangers.

Other simple annuals I like for cutting are poppies of all kinds, annual chrysanthemums, candytuft, small sunflowers, annual dianthus, linaria, and many of the 'everlasting flowers' which preserve easily. These include helichrysum, rhodanthe (with dainty white to pink daisy flowers for making into pictures and calendars as well as pleasant posies for winter days), and statice (the one called 'Pink Pokers' has long, pointed rose-pink spikes for drying). And I mustn't forget zinnias for cutting, and clary and cosmea, and mignonette, scabious and portulaca.

Gourds, too, might be started on a warm kitchen window ledge this month. Soak the seed in warm water for three days before sowing, and plant out the young seedlings when the soil feels really warm.

Getting ready for summer

With spring at last in the air, this is a good time to divide hardy border plants. Dig up the root and then, using two full-sized garden forks, place them back to back and push them into the centre of the clump which is to be split up. Firmly lever the handles apart and the clump will divide.

And now is the time I hard prune my grey-foliaged garden shrubs such as *Senecio laxifolius*, the southernwood (lad's love), by the gate, and any other shrubs which require this attention every year, like the pink-tinted berberis 'Rosy Glow'. I also remove twiggy, dead, and crossing branches from many others. All this ensures well-shaped shrubs and plenty of good long stems so useful for flower arranging. In my garden the winter-flowering daphnes, mahonias, and winter prunus get all the 'pruning' they require as they are gently cut for the house; the *Daphne mezereum* is slow to shoot again from any cut, and so must be only sympathetically gathered.

The art of re-potting

Thank goodness March is not all cold winds. We should get a little sunshine, and on such days sunrooms and conservatories will begin to warm up and make the perfect place to do a bit of indoor gardening. Dividing and re-potting of houseplants is one of the jobs I like to get on with while from the conservatory windows I can watch the garden birds and see new signs of spring every day.

'The re-potting of indoor ferns should be tackled before new growth begins to be made', I read the other day. True, but don't 'over-pot'. Putting a fern, or any other plant, from a small pot into a huge one with the aim of encouraging it to do better is not a good idea. On the contrary, like most plants the root system of the fern likes to feel the side of the pot – so simply move it up into the next size of pot, using a peat-based compost. As with all potting, it pays handsomely to

buy yourself a pack of proper potting compost rather than just filling up with soil from the garden.

If window ledge space is a problem, or you just don't want the expense of a new pot, the fern's roots can be carefully pruned back and the plant returned to its old pot with fresh compost. Or you can divide your fern into two. Other

Crocus, snowdrops, daisies and sprigs of this and that from the garden, arranged in water-retaining foam. Notice the green rose (Viridiflora) half-way up. 37

houseplants can be divided at this time too. Round about now, too, I begin to feed all my houseplants to bring them into healthy growth.

Summer potted plants

A pleasure this month is to visit a friend who is a keen member and official of one of the societies for geranium enthusiasts. Her tiny greenhouse is bliss even in March, filled with amazing colour. 'You need never be without flowers,' she tells me, 'if you grow zonal geraniums (pelargoniums), so long as you give them warmth, water, and maximum light.' Those geraniums with very colourful foliage, too, can be kept looking attractive all winter. 'Pelargoniums are not deciduous; they do not naturally lose their leaves in the winter,' says my friend. As most homes have a poor sickly geranium or two waiting for the spring before they begin growing again, this may come as a surprise. Flat dwellers in particular might like to remember it.

There are some really gloriously coloured geraniums around these days and a visit to a specialist nursery is very well worthwhile, if only to see the many kinds which produce not only desirable flowers but colourful leaves into the bargain. I admire one called 'Happy Thought' not only for its name but for its green and white leaves and another firm favourite of mine is 'Mrs Cox'; she is a brilliant beauty with foliage of Indian red, cream, and a lively green.

Gloxinia tubers are among the things I am on the lookout for this month to make summer potted plants – certainly the least expensive way to enjoy these charmers. I know gloxinias have a name for being difficult, but the problem is generally caused by over- or under-watering. Never let them dry right out, but give a good drink in a bowl of water when the soil just feels dry to the touch, then allow them to drain. I find it pays to start my tubers off in one of the soil-less vermiculites, taking care not to water the crown of the plant, which could cause it to rot off. When new growth gets under way I transfer to a six-inch (15 cm) pot containing potting compost, leaving the top of the tuber uncovered.

Another 'must do' for March is to start off some tuberous begonias in seven-inch (18 cm) pots filled almost to the top with an open potting compost, but again leaving the top of each tuber clear. These always do well for me in partial shade indoors and out, and make splendid plants for summer porch and terrace troughs and for window boxes. The larger the tuber, by the way, the greater the number of flowers you can expect. Even if you live in a high-rise flat and have only a balcony you can enjoy many flowers by using tubs, painted buckets, decorative pots, or window boxes. And these can be particularly lovely as we come into April.

Flowers in March

From the garden: Crocus, bergenia, hellebores, primroses.

From the shops: Forced lilac, tulips, daffodils, *Prunus triloba*, anemones, polyanthus, grape hyacinths, spray carnations.

APRIL

This is the weather the cuckoo likes,
And so do I;
When showers betumble the chestnut spikes,
And nestlings fly:
And the little brown nightingale bills his best,
And they sit outside at "The Travellers' Rest",
And maids come forth sprig-muslin drest,
And citizens dream of the south and west,
And so do I . . .

Thomas Hardy

April comes in with the countryside playing its age-old harmonies of tender green and brown. The swallows come, and lambs play through a mix of days of mild air or spiteful iciness. This is a golden time, with forsythia straight from the garden, and daffodils – which we all know 'come before the swallow dares' – blooming along the window boxes, down every border, and, in my corner of England, on the roadside verges and traffic islands where they have been planted by the councils and flower-minded local bodies.

The skylark sings across the meadow opposite the house. Marsh marigold, stitchwort, wild strawberry and violet will all be in flower this month. There's an old country belief that when the wild sloe (blackthorn) is in full flower, like snow along the hedgerows, a 'blackthorn winter' sets in. Certainly I have noticed that more often than not as a brief warm spell brings out the sloe blossom so there is quickly a change in the weather to biting cold, if only for a few days. So don't be tempted by a bit of early sunshine to risk tender plants out of doors prematurely.

Daffodils

Even on warm April days, winds are often a problem. In my hilltop garden, like bouncy puppies they infuriatingly snap off the long-awaited daffodils at ground level. I fill the house with the enforced harvest, gathering more and more blooms each day before rain bedraggles and snails gnaw pieces from them. Any wilted flowers and buds are soon revived by re-cutting the stem ends and standing them in a deep jug of lukewarm water for half an hour or so before arranging.

When the flowers have been broken off, as often happens, with only a few inches of stem, the only thing to do is mass the heads in a suitable dish or bowl. Keen flower arrangers, of course, don't normally mind cutting down flower stems to lengths suitable for the design they have in mind; indeed, they do it all 39

Great sprays of joyous forsythia with daffodils, very informally arranged on a pinholder in a shallow modern dish as if growing, make a homely decoration for Easter. In a busy life, informality is fine – don't worry about 'great art'!

40

the time when arranging roses, pinks, chrysanthemums, and most other things. But, somehow, it is different with a daffodil. When a daffodil loses its elegant pale green stem its special lilting airiness is lost. A daffodil, whether growing wild or captured beautifully indoors, seems to truly need its stem to show it off well, and the best arrangements follow this maxim.

Unusual varieties

Daffodils come in many rather dreamy colours, including white (like the one called 'Mount Hood'), soft butter creams, and clear yellows, with short cups and trumpets or longer ones, fluted, or streaked in wild variety. Daffodils do not have to be arranged alone, but look superb with hyacinths (pink, white, or blue), the green-yellow euphorbias, the winter blooming purple iris (*unguieularis*), and any of the clear-coloured blossoms of spring. I like a low earth-coloured dish for such a mixture, and another pleasure is to complement daffodils with yellow-edged holly, variegated privet, or long sprays of foliage from the old-fashioned roses.

Daffodils are fairly easy flowers to please, so just arrange them and enjoy them. It is worth looking out for some of the less common kinds, such as the split corona types from Holland, which are rather like unusual yellow orchids. The trumpet is strange; it grows split open as if somebody had separated it into six sections. People can't believe this is natural, but it is! Varieties include 'Golden Orchid', pale yellow petals with golden trumpet, and 'Parisienne', white petals with orange cup. Personally I like this flower very much, particularly when used in massed designs; it slips in more easily and less obtrusively than the normal trumpeting sorts. The paler yellow back petals are stained with quiet greens, which is enchanting and is also one of the reasons they are easy to blend with other colours.

The daffodils which have double trumpets are equally outstanding, and you can often buy them in the shops as cut flowers. Again the trumpet is divided, but this time with a flounced and fluted effect like the skirts of the ladies in 'Come Dancing'!

Basket containers

The gipsies who come into town now have their baskets and old perambulators filled with daffodils, and the pleasant familiar sight of the former recalls that baskets of all kinds, with or without handles, make charming containers for massed arrangements of daffodils or indeed any other flowers. A dish or bowl of some kind must be provided, of course, to hold the water (not too small, or it won't take all the stems). Use a pinholder to secure the tallest central stems, and a 'cap' of lightly crumpled chicken wire to cover the water-holder and to support the stems in the places you want them to stay. Hook a few of the straggly cut ends of wire into the basketwork for security. If the basket has a handle, leave this rather clear of flowers and leaves, so that you get the appearance of a 41

well-balanced basketful of blooms which you could pick up and walk about with. This is an important point for a show entry, if you are using such a basket as a container.

Another way is to fill the basket with spring flowers arranged with their own leaves in small, tight 'gipsy' posies. In this way you get an effect of vivid colour – and a very simple and pleasing arrangement for a table or shelf on which you look down. Such a design often looks well even standing on the floor in country fashion.

Tulips

Daffodils arrange well with those other flowers which are so essential a feature of spring for most of us – tulips. Before arranging tulips I always prick the stems under the flowerheads with a pin, to help them to drink, then wrap the bunch firmly in a few sheets of newspaper and leave them to take a long soak in a bucket for an hour or so, keeping the heads above the water, of course.

In theory, tulips should be the most perfect flowers from the arranger's point of view. They come in almost every colour, to fit in with any scheme. Their shape is pointed in bud and rounded when fully open. They last well in water. They have a very long garden season if various kinds are grown. Their foliage is fresh and green and suits them to perfection. But with all this going for them,

The garden can be a living flower arrangement, with blocks of colour used to create points of interest. Here, orange parrot tulips are teamed with azaleas.

they are not favourite flowers for arranging because they have one bad fault – they are among the few flowers I know whose stems continue growing when cut and placed in water. And those stems twist to the light and will not stay where you put them in any formal design.

Fortunately, not all tulips suffer from this 'fault' to quite the same extent as the long-stemmed early singles and the May-flowering Darwins. The paeony-flowered, the early doubles, and others grown sturdily in the open garden are not nearly so difficult to arrange.

Bulb flowers

One of the pleasures of April is a walk in the garden to enjoy the hyacinths. I plant more each year for their big scented heads, but the smaller flowers which were originally forced for the house, before being planted out, are specially noteworthy for a little mixed posy. So don't forget to transfer to the garden all your winter forced indoor bulbs.

Other bulb flowers which I plant for cutting this month include the giant Crown Imperial, which smells of foxes when disturbed. Each great flower bell when turned upside down can be seen to hold a 'tear'. Tradition has it that when the flower refused to bow its head as Jesus passed to His crucifixion it became so distressed that it has ever since carried a tear in each of its crown-like blooms.

Sir Cecil Beaton, flower arranger

Tubs of blue grape hyacinth in the conservatory and the double white arabis edging garden paths make me think of the late Sir Cecil Beaton's house at Broad Chalke in Wiltshire. When I went to see him, a trough of blue grape hyacinths greeted me at the door, and I took him a nosegay of small flowers which included this arabis. 'Sir Cecil enjoys having flowers everywhere,' said his secretary, walking me through the cool marbled entrance hall to meet him in the library. Long sprays of delicate white spring blossoms cascaded from a Picasso 'figure' pot in a window, and large floor-standing tubs and baskets held an exuberant display of indoor plants. There was an orange tree full of oranges, an enormous flouncing pale pink pelargonium, many superb green foliage plants. Outdoors, daffodils in massed, packed colour could be seen through a green clipped archway.

'When he was in London all week,' Sir Cecil's secretary went on, 'he would arrive here about eleven o'clock on Friday mornings and almost before he had taken off his coat would go round the garden with basket and secateurs, perhaps making up to four visits before he had filled all the vases, large and small, in all the rooms. His arrangements are totally individual – I have never met anyone who arranges flowers as he does.'

On the day of my visit there were certainly flowers everywhere, indoors and out. I was invited to see Sir Cecil's flower room, with its rows of pegs holding his well-known collection of hats, and its shelves full of containers of all kinds. A 43

handsome eighteenth-century Delft ware tulip vase of blue and white, which Sir Cecil loved to arrange with pink, green, and white flowers, rubbed shoulders with a Victorian jug painted with roses, other striking pots made by Picasso, and a large selection of simple glass vases. He particularly liked to use strong leaf shapes and bold flowers that have attractive stems 'so that they shine through glass' – he told me he didn't like 'anything niminy-piminy'.

White flowers were his great favourite, and they abounded both indoors and out. He had exciting cutting borders filled in summer with delphiniums, dahlias, and paeonies. In summer, Sir Cecil said, there were trails of 'Caroline Testout' roses on the balustrade and romantic garlands (made of rope, on which the flowers are trained) of pink 'Dr. Van Fleet' roses, and scented flowers filled the terraces in a muted wash of colour.

Indoors again, I admired a single orchid in a tall container on his desk and an informal arrangement of moon-yellow narcissus in pewter on the dining table, making fine harmony with the old Peruvian terracotta displayed in the room. The dining room I found almost monastic in its restrained decor, in contrast with the rest of the house where flowers were placed everywhere, arranged extremely simply and with great charm as specimens or en masse. They all looked easy on the eye and completely at home as arranged by the hand of this master designer.

It is lovely to be able to arrange flowers well for all occasions, but the lesson to be learned from Sir Cecil's house, it seemed to me, was that unless we are arranging flowers for competition or a festival, wedding or other special occasion, the best designs for home are always those which fit in informally, being not too much on their dignity and so in tune with today's free and easy life-styles. There is no need, ever, to apologise as many women do for the soft, untailored, casually 'unarranged' look of flowers in the home – these often have great appeal and invididuality. Sir Cecil reinforced my view, too, that both antique and modern containers go well anywhere so long as they seem to link with their immediate surroundings.

The different kinds of flower arranging

I find it interesting that flower arranging is beginning to slip into four clear divisions:

1. The wonderfully inspiring exemplary effects so cleverly displayed by countless skilled demonstrators at flower arrangement club meetings. Many women find it now difficult to actually copy some of these because of the price of flowers and the smallness of most modern gardens. But they are a great delight to see.

2. The superb designs created for flower festivals and the like in cathedrals, churches, and stately homes, with each arrangement planned to exactly suit its particular position. Many thousands of pounds are raised every year for charities by these festivals.

Dappled sunlight catches a Victorian child's wheelbarrow used as a container for small spring flowers. Many imaginative containers can be used outside.

A bunch of fresh parsley from a market stall arranged in a simple pottery basket looks attractive as it keeps crisp on the kitchen window ledge.

3. Competitive flower arranging, which really pulls out all the stops to achieve perfection, distinction and to conform exactly to the requirements laid down in the show schedule.

4. Home flower arrangements which are easy on the eye, quick to achieve, informal. Few women today seem to have time to do the flowers in the manner to which we have become accustomed in the last twenty years or so. Most of us have not only to run our homes but do jobs as well. I know many competent arrangers, and these include famed demonstrators, judges and teachers of the art, who are beginning to say 'I never have time to do the flowers at home'. So, at home, keep the flower designs extremely simple – but do the occasional big formal arrangement just to keep your hand in. And do remember that not every flower arrangement has to be a time-consuming work of art. A few sprays of blossom in a jug, a garden gathering of stock displayed in a child's mug, can be very pretty. Have confidence, enjoy the flowers for themselves and never make excuses for a flower decoration because of its simplicity.

Church flowers at Easter

On Easter Saturday, churches big and small up and down the land are awash with ladies 'doing the flowers'. Last year I spent the day driving round my neighbouring small towns and villages just to see the flowers in the various churches and chapels, and I found that every place of worship's flower arrangements had its own special feeling and character. One church has very sensibly kept a big circular Victorian trough container, with a built-in series of 45

tubes hanging from it which exactly fits the font; it is brought out, they told me, every Easter and quickly, easily, filled with brilliant flowers giving the effect of a circle of colour with slim trails of flowers falling from it.

At another church they had a gorgeous blue-grey painted backdrop for the Easter garden, made from fine butter muslin with lighting behind it. What struck me in all the churches as remarkable was that none of the arrangers thought they were doing anything unusual. That the decorations were unique to their own church, with something quite different going on at the church down the road, had not occurred to them. In one church I found they were making circlets of fresh leaves for the top of every pillar; at another, the bases of the choir stalls were decorated with tulips imaginatively grouped with their own leaves just as though they were growing.

Another church had a standard apple tree in full blossom (growing in a tub) by the altar, with daffodils and little spring flowers at its foot, again as if growing. In this last rather plain tailored country church the effect was entrancing, completely 'different', yet utterly in keeping. The arranger told me she had tired of formal pedestals, which seemed too similar. 'I bought the tree from a nursery, and I'll plant it in my garden after Easter,' she explained. 'Next year, I'll think of something else.'

Doing the church flowers

I know many women are nervous if they are asked to help with church flowers, but there's no need to get sick with worry. The great thing, of course, is just to do one's best, but over the years I have gathered from experience a few tips which will help. The first thing you need to take into account is whether your allotted position is dark or light. In a not-too-light situation, use light-reflecting colours, such as white, cream, primrose, pale pinks, and apricot, rather than deeper blues, browns, greens, even oranges and reds, which will simply disappear, particularly if they are placed against dark church woodwork. The reverse often applies if your flowers are to be seen in strong light against the background of a light-coloured stone or concrete wall. Because church arrangements are invariably set in large spaces, bold clean-cut flowers are the best choice, or you can create blocks of colour with clusters of smaller blooms.

If there are no 'old hands' involved with you, you may have to check beforehand on whether suitable containers, pinholders, chicken wire, and so on, are already available at the church, and also on such points as where the Vicar likes the flowers. For example, some clergy do not permit flowers on the altar; others prefer it if no flowers are arranged to stand higher than the altar cross, which they believe should always be the most prominent symbol. If you are using garden flowers, pick them the day before you have to arrange them, and give them a deep drink in a cool place overnight. Bought flowers, too, should have stem ends re-cut and then deep overnight drinks before you start

arranging them.

*Bunched polyanthus gathered from a
spring border arranged with a light-
hearted spray of ivy. A handsome
natural sea-shell is the container.*

Church vases

One problem you may come across is that of coping with the thin-waisted brass
altar vases which seem to have been acquired by churches in their thousands in
Victorian times. I have found that the best way is to use Oasis. Divide the
flowers and foliage into two lots, then place the two altar vases side by side and
arrange them as a complementary pair. Place your tallest stem first towards the 47

centre back of one vase, then place a matching stem in the other. Continue matching them as you work; for the sides choose branches or stems which have built-in bends or curves to them. Short sprays, perhaps of ivy which grows naturally in a flowing manner, might be placed so that they come down over the front to soften the hard rim of the vase.

Sometimes we are allowed to take our own containers; bowls, urns, or anything dignified in shape, colour, and general character, or which will be totally hidden by the flowers and leaves in the finished arrangement. Working with a familiar container is often helpful, but if you really do have to cope with the well-polished, treasured Victorian altar vase you may find it helpful to cap the whole thing with chicken wire to support the stems. Or perhaps you could insert into the neck of the vase a candlecup or a funnel (suitably painted) containing the damp floral foam. This would make it possible to have a wider, more flowing design.

Flowers at home

This month there are so many lovely things in bloom which are just right for homely flower arrangements. Subjects like Soldiers and Sailors, whose proper name is *Pulmonaria officinalis*, and whose other interesting old country names are lungwort and spotted dog.

The name Soldiers and Sailors, by the way, comes about because the plant bears both pink and blue flowers at the same time (resembling old-time uniforms). The name lungwort refers to the lung-like blotching of the leaves, and in fact the plant is so old that it goes back to times when people thought every plant which resembled some part of the body had been put on earth to help cure that part when it got sick. As for spotted dog, well, look at the leaf.

Then there are tiny bulb flowers and country celandines, chequered snake's head fritillary, and primroses. Many are flowers and leaves which will not put up with being arranged in water-retaining foams but prefer clear deep water.

About now the indoor raised sweet peas and chrysanthemums can be planted out and when the forsythia has finished flowering we can prune it.

And then, hooray, we're into May!

Flowers in April

From the garden: Daphne, daffodils, polyanthus, primroses, early rhododendrons, bleeding heart (dicentra), tulips, dusty millers (auriculas), apple blossom.

From the shops: Bulbous iris, lilies, tulips, and a wealth of Spring flowers.

MAY

Your hands lie open in the long fresh grass, –
Your finger-points look through like rosy blooms;
Your eyes smile peace. The pasture gleams and glooms,
'Neath billowing skies that scatter and amass.
All round our nest, far as the eye can pass,
Are golden kingcup-fields with silver edge
Where the cow-parsley skirts the hawthorn-hedge . . .

Dante Gabriel Rossetti

The lovely month of May slips in with the crowning of the May Queens, and bluebells, buttercups, and wild lupins out at last along wooded country lanes. The chestnut trees in the Park of the Castle, which I can just see through my front windows, come into full candle flower, and velvet bees plunge knee-deep into cherry, lime, peach, and young apple blossom. This is a time of richness and plenty, with lilac, wallflower, meadowsweet, and lily of the valley scenting the air in town and village gardens.

In London, the great tents go up for the Chelsea Flower Show, while I pick Queen Anne's lace along the lane for a wedding in the local church, and a sudden cool shower sends the sheep to shelter under hedges sprigged pink and white with early May blossom.

In the town the market traders are out in force with their neat rows of boxed bedding plants, and somehow, we probably all fall for a new plant or two in May. Even on the wet days the lightness in the air fills us with ideas for making our immediate surroundings more interesting, alive, and in tune with the season. But it would really be best if we could contain our enthusiasm for a little longer, closer to the end of the month or even into June if we live in the north. By then ill tempered overnight frosts are less likely, and the bracing spring winds which check the growth of young plants have had time to calm down and warm up. Don't risk young plants out of doors too soon; cosy them along in the shelter of a porch, conservatory, or cold frame for a week or two.

Planting up the spring flowers

My first buys usually go to filling the porch afresh, as the earlier polyanthus and hyacinths go over. I buy one or two geraniums, a petunia, or a half-box of pansies each week. Close at hand, I find, petunias and pansies have a soft elusive perfume. All the too-early-to-be-outdoors plants intended for summer bedding make lovely temporary pot plants for the house. I have an antique china wash- 49

hand basin which I bought from a market junk stall. With three big double pink or single white petunias it makes a rather money-no-object-looking decoration for the dining table, though I have to move it out of the way at mealtimes!

Any similar plants can be put into potting compost in bulb bowls, tureens, pretty jars, or other suitable containers.

The big velvet pansies, like Edwardian hat decorations, are impossible to pass by without buying one or two. The large named ones are usually sold individually. They are perfectly hardy and can go into the garden quite early. They look good planted in profusion in terrace pots; a planting of all one colour in each pot looks best, to my eye. Again, they make charming temporary pot plants for the house, although generally you will find that they need an immediate re-potting.

Frivolous hanging baskets, lined with moss, and window boxes can be planted up now and kept growing steadily away under cover in a light place such as the sunroom, so that by the time they are to go into their summer positions they will be positively billowing with flowers. To water a wire hanging basket, take it down and submerge the whole thing in a washing-up bowl of water until the bubbles stop rising. Stand it on a bucket to drain. Give a feed once a week.

By this time some of my hardy border plants are already in a fine flurry of flower. Among a host which come up to greet us like dear old friends are the little rock plants like variegated aubrietia, iberis, and golden alyssum. All are useful for arranging in small containers such as boxes, wine glasses, and the like. The wallflowers, forget-me-nots, and lunaria (honesty) make a splash of colour and remind me that it is almost time to sow more of them, for being biennials it will take a year for them to flower from seed sown now.

Preserving spring flowers

Both wallflowers and forget-me-nots preserve perfectly in a drying medium called silica gel, to make enchanting decorations for Christmas cards and calendars or to be framed in dried flower pictures. You can buy silica gel crystals from the larger chemists' shops, where it is sold as a drying agent for keeping lawnmowers and other equipment free of damp during winter storage. Silica gel and similar drying mediums can also be obtained in powder form, with more difficulty perhaps, but they are less likely to pock-mark delicate petals. Sales tables at flower arrangement clubs are the most likely places to find the powders, though some departmental stores stock named products. Many different leaves, flowers and buds can be preserved including violets, crocus, polyanthus and aconites, but they must be dry and in perfect condition before you begin.

Place them individually face up in a box containing about one inch of the substance, and gently cover them by trickling more crystals or the powder over them. Carry on building up layers in this way; the top layer must be the drying agent. Leave the box in a warm place until the flowers are crisp, then take them out and store them, in another box, in a dry place until you wish to use them.

The sculptor Barbara Hepworth's Cornish garden in late May has much to teach a flower arranger about the contrasts of light and dark.

Next year's cinerarias

Gardeners and flower arrangers are always looking ahead, and I like to sow a pinch or two of flowering primula and cineraria seed this month. The wide-eyed starry daisy flowers of the cineraria, in their unbelievably gorgeous hues, came originally from the Canary Islands, and I find them irresistible. In fact, I usually make a second sowing in June to give me plenty of flowers with which to fill my small conservatory next spring. To see them blooming on a grey February day, or perhaps against a background of snow, is reward indeed for a little forethought in May and June.

Other people's gardens

Talk of cinerarias takes me to happy lazy holidays spent in May at St Ives in Cornwall, for there in the milder air these plants seed and come through the winter, producing startling drifts of colour under the windswept trees in the public gardens, where they have been allowed to naturalise. When you have 51

only ever thought of a cineraria as a rather prim pot plant the sight is as stimulating as it is unexpected.

A lovely once-private garden now open to the public is that of the late Barbara Hepworth, the sculptor whose studios it surrounds. One does not have to understand modern sculpture to enjoy this garden which she created and loved. It is set high up in the old town, within sight and sound of the sea. Here the shrubs in flower and the early roses intermingle, flouncing and cascading around the bold smooth shapes of cliff-like sculptures. Utterly memorable are the sharp pinks, clear calm blues, and crisp white cineraria flowers as they are occasionally glimpsed through the caverns and clefts which are so typical of Barbara Hepworth's work.

Seeing what other people have been up to is always a source of enormous interest to gardeners. A year or two ago I went along when Beverley Nichols threw open his cottage and garden at Ham Common in Surrey. The cottage is a large one, and after admiring the tiny front paved garden with its small lead figure we went through an archway into the walled garden complete with urns, pond, trees, and mature plants about which Mr Nichols has written so entertainingly. It was a hot day, but indoors the music room was cool with its tall shelves of books and grand piano. Mr Nichols had done elegant arrangements of cream and pale pink flowers, and there were stocks, paeonies, and roses

Above: In a cottage dining room, a gently massed arrangement in a basket with an inner container for the water.

Right: Flowers for a new baby girl are realistic silk pinks, arranged with real wallflowers and foliage or epimedium.

52

in huge silver wine coolers which stood on handsome pieces of antique furniture in front of high gilt-framed mirrors. The effect was magical, as was the informally arranged parsley with daisies in a white-painted basket which stood in the hearth, while in the dining room dandelion clocks and leaves intrigued the unknowing. (The secret of dandelion clocks is to give them a light spray with hair lacquer to preserve them and stop them blowing away.)

Flowers and saints

In days gone by many common flowers were dedicated to favourite saints, and often the pet name of a plant echoes this. Flowers in bloom around the saint's special day were gathered and used for decorating the church, often being strewn over the altar. St George's Day sees the wild slender-stemmed harebell in flower, and so it is dedicated to him. St John has St John's Wort (hypericum), St Barnabas the midsummer or ox-eye daisy, and St Michael the michaelmas daisy. To St Agnes belongs the Christmas rose, and the cowslip used to be known as St Peter's wort, for the clusters of blossom were said to resemble a bunch of keys, the apostle's symbol.

The great white lily (*Lilium candidum*), the Madonna lily, has long been associated with the Virgin Mary, as is the marigold (Mary gold), and lady's mantle (*Alchemilla mollis*), that special favourite with flower arrangers for its

green star flowers and pleated leaves. Then there are lady's smock, lady fern, and the Virgin's bower clematis.

Gardens were devoted to growing flowers for the church, and one such adjoining the Lady Chapel at Winchester Cathedral was called Paradise. In his will, Henry VI left directions concerning a garden for the church of Eton College to grow 'trees and flowers for the service of the said church'.

When we are decorating our own parish churches it would be pleasant to search out the special flower of the patron saint and make at least one arrangement with it. St Augustine's Day falls in May, for example, and to him is dedicated the rhododendron. St Philip's flower is the red tulip, and St James's the red campion.

Seasonal favourites

Favourite flowers change with the seasons, but without doubt my favourite of May and June is *Dicentra spectabilis*, the plant with so many country names – Jingling Johnny, Bleeding heart, Dutchman's breeches, and Lady's locket among them. Any plant with so many nicknames has been popular for a long time, we can be sure, and in fact it was first introduced to Britain in 1816 and became widely known and dearly loved in Victorian times, particularly for potting and bringing indoors to force for early flowers. (And, incidentally, Dicentra leaves and flowers last well when cut.)

Bleeding heart, Lady's locket, and Dutchman's breeches are all fairly obvious names once you see this plant in flower. But I often wondered, why Jingling Johnny? And then one day I happened to notice an advertisement for porcelain figures of early nineteenth-century soldiers. In the centre, a coloured boy soldier in a bright uniform carried a sort of parasol with bells attached to it. He, I discovered, was a 'Jingling Johnny', who marched at the head of a regimental band shaking his jingling 'umbrella' in time to the music and tossing it high in the air. The newly-introduced dicentra flowers were seen to resemble the little bells, hence 'Jingling Johnny'.

If for nothing else, though, this flower would endear itself to me because of yet another pet name, 'Lady in the bath'. Gently open the two pink spurs at the side of each new opening flower and you can see the small white lady sitting in her bath.

The massed arrangement

With such a wealth of plant material in the garden this month, and coming more cheaply into the shops, now is the time to try a massed arrangement. This is just what it sounds like – an arrangement using a mass of flowers. Obviously, a reasonably wide-topped container is required; this could be an oval vegetable tureen, or a box perhaps with a container inside for water, or anything of pleasing shape and suitable size will do. One of my own most useful flower holders is a very large plastic plant pot saucer which becomes quite hidden

54

under its mass of flowers and leaves when the design is complete. These saucers come in all sizes and of course I use smaller saucers for smaller arrangements.

To hold the stems you need a pinholder and a piece of two-inch (50 mm) mesh chicken wire of a size which, crumpled up loosely, fills the container and stands

Pieris Forrestii *'Forest Flame' is a superb shrub for an arranger, with spring foliage which looks like heads of flowers; it needs a hot water drink.* 55

just a little higher than its rim. Crossing two rubber bands or some clear sticky tape right round, as if round a parcel, will hold the chicken wire firmly in place.

Position the container where you want it to be displayed, and almost fill it with tepid water to which you can add, if you like, a teaspoonful of sugar or a packet of flower food called Chrysal. Now go ahead with the arrangement, threading the stems of flowers and leaves through the chicken wire into the water; the wire will hold everything in place, from thin-stalked Bachelor's Buttons (the perennial garden ranunculus of early summer) to the thick stems of paeonies. Gather two main shapes: long, slim, pointed things like budding iris or sprays of beech for making the outline, and rounder, fuller shapes like opening roses, poppies etc for the centre heart of the design. Things mid-way between the two are needed for 'fillers' and all arrangements look better for foliage to create what Constance Spry once called 'an oasis of calm between the flowers'. In competitive work many a lovely design is spoiled because it lacks a few good plain leaf shapes as a foil between the patterning of many flowers.

To make the favourite basic triangular design, begin by defining the silhouette or outline shape, cutting a tall branch or flower stem approximately one-and-a-half times to twice the height of your container. (But if the container is a very shallow bowl or dish, the tallest stem should be measured to one-and-a-half to twice the width.) Place it in position towards the centre back of the container, impaling it through the wire and on to the pinholder. Next put in two side stems, low down. These should be cut about the same length as each other. Put in one at each side. When you have sketched in your outline put in your principal, boldest, flowers and well-shaped leaves at the centre front, just above rim level. Fill in with other flowers and leaves, grading them as you go, keeping all within the triangle formed by the first three placements. It is all much easier than it sounds!

I must say I like to keep the old country names alive. We are all learning more of the correct botanical names while the traditional ones sadly get less known. The Latin names are important when ordering plants from nurserymen (otherwise you may not get the things you actually want), but what a pleasure it is to know that the garden plant called astrantia (the botanical title is an allusion to the star-like flowerheads, says the Royal Horticultural Society's *Dictionary of Gardening*) used to be called Hattie's pincushion years ago. Why? Just because that is how it looks. An excellent variety for use as a foliage plant in flower arranging is *Astrantia maxima* 'Variegata', and it is at perfection this month.

May is a treasure of a month . . . but June, with its roses scenting the summer evenings, should be even better.

Flowers in May
From the garden: Lily-of-the-valley, columbine, lilac, prunus, snake's head lily (fritillaria), bishop's hat (epimedium), tulips, azaleas, and Solomon's seal.

JUNE

There is sweet music here that softer falls
Than petals from blown roses on the grass . . .
Here are cool mosses deep,
And thro' the moss the ivies creep,
And in the stream the long-leaved flowers weep,
And from the craggy ledge the poppy hangs in sleep.
Alfred, Lord Tennyson

June, the month when clumps of scarlet field poppies, and moon-pennies with their golden eyes, flounce for miles over the undisturbed banks of the ever-pounding motorways. In the quiet of my lane, few cars pass the dog-rose and honeysuckle, baby hazelnut and swelling haw, and in the park by the castle the chestnuts have infant conkers already. Conservatory and porch smell of white petunia and stock.

Rose shows come and go, seeding grasses send the hay fever sufferers sneezing indoors, and cottage gardens are filled with bearded iris, rose, scabious, delphinium, periwinkle, campanula, fast-budding lily. A month of butterflies, curtains fluttering in wide-open windows, foxgloves, strawberries and cream, the first garden raspberries. There is a profusion of flowers in the garden and, for the flower arranger, June is perhaps the crowning month of the whole year.

The time of roses
Above all, it is the time of roses. Mine is a hilltop garden and the roses tend to be late coming out, but always among the earliest in June are the old-fashioned ones. There are the Victorian-looking moss roses, with buds set thick with green mossing, and the cerise-pink Zephirine Drouhin, the thornless rose, which provides a delicious old-world perfume. During the early part of the month I envy people with milder garden conditions. For me, foxgloves, forget-me-nots, and hardy geraniums provide colour among the budding roses, and I look each day to see which will be the first rose to come out, for the flowering of the roses is the arrival of summer.

Suddenly they come, wave upon wave. The climbers are generally first. The velvety 'Guinea', on the south front of the house, catches the sun early and bursts into blood-red bloom. The clear yellow 'Golden Showers' which I used to grow up an apple tree in my last garden, starts slowly at first in this garden but flowers over a long period on the archway leading to the orchard.

I cannot mention many of the 500 roses I grow, but one or two are specially noteworthy. First the early-blooming single 'Frühlingsmorgen' (Spring Morning), like a large wild rose almost, which is why I have it in the front garden against a backdrop of the fields and oak trees across the lane. Although not normally thought of as worth growing for its hips, I find them big and splendid and most useful in late arrangements. Then there is tiny Cécile Brunner, which delights everyone. It makes quite a big bush but is perfection in bud, and gives a profusion of perfectly formed miniature pink blooms like the ones my grandmother had painted on her best china teacups. For an excellent off-beat red I would recommend Rosemary Rose, a good long-lasting flower when cut, with a neat old-fashioned air which appeals to flower arrangers.

A group of roses of which I am extremely fond are those in the collection named after characters in *The Canterbury Tales*, produced as a result of crossing old-fashioned varieties with modern hybrid tea roses. The Knight is like a crimson carnation, the Yeoman ruddily pink as if he has been out in the fresh air all day, Chaucer is an unusual clear delicate pink double, and the Prioress (my own favourite) is quietly pale and interesting. She does, however, make strong and healthy growth. These roses combine the buttony, quartered, and divided petal formation of the old roses with the ability to bloom a second time each season, which the true 'old-fashioneds' don't often possess.

The old roses

The old-fashioned roses are renowned for their fresh simplicity and I would always try to include one in even the smallest garden. As well as the damasks, musks, and centifolias I love the fifteenth-century Maiden's Blush, the Jacobite Rose (*alba maxima*), the 'velvet rose' Tuscany, and of course the old cabbage rose.

These old roses are specially linked with the Empress Josephine of France. Her great passion for gardening and for roses came to its peak at Malmaison for which she spent a fortune on plants and financed expeditions abroad. Even though Britain was at war with France, the Prince Regent gave orders that any plants intercepted at sea by our ships were to be allowed safe passage to her.

Appropriately, the Empress was born in the rosy month of June and her second Christian name too was Rose. The year after her death, Napoleon visited her old garden. 'How the spirit of Josephine pervades this place,' he said. 'How graceful she was . . . I can almost see her walking in the garden among the flowers.' Published two years later was the famous book *Les Roses* for which Josephine had commissioned the artist Redouté to paint all the roses she grew in her garden. We are still enjoying her roses and his pictures of them today.

Coming up to date, I will always associate roses with the Queen Mother who is a great rose-lover and almost every year she is to be seen at the Royal National Rose Society show. I well remember seeing her when I used to exhibit flower
arrangements there. This rather shy lady used always to make a special point of

pausing by the displays of old-fashioned roses to smell their sweetness and talk to the growers. And, of course, she has a rose named after her 'Elizabeth of Glamis'. It is a lovely salmon-pink-to-orange floribunda, which is deliciously fragrant and full-flowering.

Trellis-patterned wallpaper suggests a rural outdoor theme for an arrangement of wild strawberries (gently carried home from a country walk). Tiny roses and seedheads link up the colour. The container is home-made.

59

June

Rose arrangements

Roses are wonderful to arrange for they come in such a wide variation of shapes, sizes and colours. There are miniatures so petite that you could pack a bunch in a big matchbox, and the large blousy ones such as Peace are ideal for cathedral-size arrangements. Roses come in sprays, clusters, and certain kinds produce perfect long-stemmed blooms if you disbud them. By disbudding, that is, removing the two side buds from a stem which has three, you leave the one main bud to develop. I can never bear to disbud my roses and in any case, I never have the time. This means that I often get a group of three flowers which open at different times on the same stem and admittedly this can be difficult when it comes to doing an arrangement for the house. I get round the problem by picking the central blooms as they open and arranging them together with their leaves in a shallow bowl with their heads just above water. The effect is positively opulent!

Another way is to make a mound of damp water-retaining foam, such as Oasis, to come just above the rim of the container. Place a frill of rose leaves round the edge and fill up the centre with the short-stemmed roses – like a garden party hat. A container on a stem is particularly good for this as it shows the flowers off with a flourish. This kind of arrangement is economical of flowers, too.

Sprays of roses look good in a tall container – something strong and earthy, perhaps in modern pottery. Arrange the flowers easily and informally, but remember that you have to remove all the thorns if chicken wire is being used, to prevent them snagging. This is easy – simply rub the back of your flower scissors vigorously up and down the stem and at the same time you can take off the lower leaves.

If you want to do a really speedy arrangement, place the stems straight into water. But ideally, an overnight deep drink is the thing.

Roses are best cut when the buds are very close to opening or just open, and in the cool of the day. Doubles last longer than singles, which in fact is the way with most flowers.

Handling shrubs

Among many handsome shrubs on hand to arrange this month are the lilacs and rhododendrons. After choosing your stems, remove most of the foliage; this makes them easier to arrange and emphasises the lovely flower. The too-heavy foliage is not particularly attractive and removing it also helps the flower to take up water, an important point with both lilacs and rhododendrons. It is essential to slice open and scrape the stem ends and give them a pre-arrangement drink in shallow boiling water. Then soak for an hour or so in deeper cool water. This may sound a bore but it works wonders. It is also an advantage to leave airy expanses of water in the container when doing the arrangement – don't pack in too many flowers – in order to provide enough humidity for the blooms.

Design for a day in high summer, using garden flowers in lighthearted mixture so that the borders hardly seem to miss them. The airy outline is made with a variety of pointed shapes which carry the eye into the main rounded flowers in the design. When using a basket with a handle, leave the handle showing.

Iris

In my garden, June is also the month of the beautiful bearded iris. These like a well-drained border in the sun, and so thoroughly enjoy life on my gravelly soil. The flowers are as unbelievable as their names. Who wouldn't fall for Laced Lemonade (yellow with lacy edges to the petals), Golden Spice (clear yellow and ginger-brown), Green Jungle (chartreuse-green flushed softly with a delicate crimson), Demon (maroon-black with a blue beard), and Green Spot (white with a bright green bit at the end of the beard)?

Possibly no other flower offers such wide variety of colours, making possible some fantastic arrangements. The stiff unbending stems are easy to arrange 61

simply by cutting them to differing lengths and impaling them on a pinholder, but I also like iris as additions to massed arrangements. As each bloom 'goes over', another bud generally opens to take its place. By the way, many iris carry the scent of vanilla about the room – or is it a lemon-like fragrance?

Dahlias

This month the dahlias can be put into the garden, a great relief if you have had them hanging around 'sprutting' since February or March. Some shelter from the wind is an advantage with dahlias, and a necessity for the taller-growing kinds. Those which need to be staked should have their props put in with them at planting time. It is worth remembering that dahlias can make pleasant plantings for tubs and window boxes. For this purpose you need the dwarf bedding varieties, and I have found 'Red Flash', 'Park Princess', and 'Fascination' especially good. Slugs and snails are as fond of dahlias as are flower arrangers! Protect with slug pellets.

Pieces of driftwood placed together on a shaped wood base make a pleasant setting for a showpiece of roses, Hattie's Pincushion, and hop foliage.

One of Britain's top dahlia men is my friend Roger Aylett, of Ayletts Gold Medal Dahlias. I asked him for the favourites in various colours used by the competitors who take part in his annual Dahlia Festival at St Albans, and this is the very comprehensive list he came up with, arranged by colours:

Peach, 'Biddenham Peach', 'Happy Birthday', 'Wee Joy', 'Lyn Mayo'.

Lilac pink, 'Monk Mark', 'Good Intent'.

Pink, 'Frank Hornsey', 'Gay Princess', 'Swiss Miss'.

Scarlet, 'Joe's Choice', 'Brigadoon', 'John Street', 'Red Flash'.

Carmine, 'Pontiac', 'Polly Peachum', 'Rothesay Robin'.

Gold/orange, 'Hugh Mather', 'Frank Hornsey', 'Highgate Gold', 'September Morn', 'Dr. Grainger'.

Soft pink, 'Diana Austin', 'Gerrie Hoek', 'Susannah York'.

Tall and handsome

Although Dutch iris are around in the June garden, don't forget the flowering eremurus, or fox-tail lilies, which are more unusual and can be invaluable for large splendid arrangements. I have special memories of them when flower clubs had a flower festival at Farnborough Hill in Hampshire, the home in this country of the Empress Eugenie of France when she was exiled. Eremurus were arranged with rose-red rhododendron on the grand piano in the music room. The setting, with the room's original faded pink silk wall coverings embossed with musical instruments, made the arrangement fitting and memorable.

Gladioli catch the eye in the flower shop windows. They are best bought – or picked for that matter – when only two or three of the florets are open. If you buy gladioli for a special occasion do arrange to have them a few days beforehand so that you can ensure a good number of the blooms are out. There is nothing more disappointing than going to pick up flowers ordered from the florist and finding them still just tight green budded sticks.

Climbing and trailing

Newly cut grass and the heavy perfumes of stock and old-fashioned flowers such as heliotrope, mignonette and lilies intermingle on the warm afternoon air, and there is the scent of the early honeysuckle on the arch over the pathway.

Plants to run up walls and poles, trellises and arches, are enormously valuable to the gardener with little space, and in a larger plot they add variety. Even edible crops can be decorative. The ordinary runner bean, for example, with its red or pink flowers, can be a picture on a green trellis against a white wall. I had the idea some years ago of planting a pink *Clematis montana* and a wistaria to scramble together up the trunk and through the boughs of an elderly prunus. The falls of purple wistaria follow the pale clematis into flower along its branches, and trails of both are encouraged to flow down romantically towards the path, so that this month the effect is rather fine. I prune the wistaria back in late winter and shorten the side shoots in August.

 **June**

An unsung plant, which deserves better, is privet. This month unclipped bushes of privet on the main road by the inn are in full bloom. Recently opened from buds which come like clusters of little white grapes, the flowers have a distinctive perfume. Customers sitting out of doors under the green and white striped parasols these sunny evenings probably wonder where the sweet scent is coming from. Few people are aware that privet, if left unclipped and allowed to grow a bit wild and free, will not only flower but fruit. A few sprigs add a surprisingly choice touch to a flower arrangement. Later in the summer the jet-black berries come in, lovely for petite-sized arrangements. Pick a bit of privet in flower for your designs, remove the foliage, and see how it intrigues people.

Tying in with the background

Arranging flowers and leaves, even fruits, to stand close by a favourite picture is always enjoyable. If exactly the right link-up of flowers and foliage can be contrived, harmonising in scale, colour and general feeling for the subject, results can be very exciting. For example, I like to put a silver jug of big blue and purple pansies in the hall under a portrait of a young Georgian miss in a dress of dark blue silk. In the dining room a stem of orange lilies stands near a local artist's painting of the town just down the hill, the colour of the flowers perfectly echoing the Georgian brickwork.

Textures, too, can often play a part. But it may only be possible to achieve a really perfect link-up once or twice a year, when suitable plant material is in season. Matching or contrasting an arrangement with the curtains, cushions, bedcovers and so on, in a room, is another challenge to ingenuity and an excuse to walk round the garden looking for just the right things to gather.

I have found that if I pick poppies in bud they open quickly indoors, and then if left undisturbed will last for days. The annual Shirley poppies are specially appealing arranged just as they are, two or three stems together in a bud vase, but the fat cottage garden border poppies (*Papaver orientale*), which come up every year, look handsome arranged in a splendid way in a large modern cherub container. This stands in the dining-room window against a backdrop of green outdoor foliage. As the tree-filtered sunlight gets round to this window the near transparent petals take on fine new highlights.

Flowers large and small

Many kinds of arrangements are possible this month with flowers of all sizes readily available. The garden paths are edged with bright pink and white thrift, and the red valerian at the gate will now also be putting up a fine show on Cornish cliffs. Thrift must surely get its name from the ease with which every small piece can be persuaded to root. Buy one tuft in a pot and within the space of two or three summers you can get enough to edge a garden path. The flowers, picked for indoors, mix in effectively with other cottage garden bits such as sprigs of lavender, sweet william, annual phlox and so on.

A traditional English arrangement of flowers and seedheads and pretty foliage. Each flower is seen to perfection in its own setting of leaves, not cramped and overcrowded. The modern container links with the backing.

65

June

Then there are the seedpods. It seems odd to think of arranging seedpods in June, but there are lots of interesting ones around this month to gather and to arrange either green and fresh, or to dry for winter designs. Bluebell spikes, primrose and polyanthus rosettes, fluffy heads of early clematis and, for miniature arrangements, the tiny lorgnette-like seedheads of spent golden alyssum, all come to mind and to hand. On a stroll round the garden I make a small gathering of my double pink soapwort (*Saponaria officinalis*). This is growing under the trails of the silver-leaf weeping pear (*Pyrus salicifolia pendula*) among pink and lavender roses and flowers on into September. Soapwort is also called by the amusing country name of 'Bouncing Bet' because, every gardener should be warned, this attractive plant does tend to bounce around not only in her own rightful bed but stealthily takes in other adjacent ones too. The leaves of soapwort were once used as soap and when I visited Uppark, the superb National Trust house near Petersfield, they told me how this plant had been used to clean and restore the colours of the hangings and covers of the bed slept in by the Prince Regent as well as the house's original window curtains, which date from 1750 and are still in use.

The question of wild flowers

A lady who is a professional illustrator of flowers and plants tells me that lanes which she remembers only twenty years ago being set with bee orchids and primroses now have none at all. Such is the worsening plight of our wild flowers, even though it is now absolutely illegal to uproot any wild plant, with a heavy fine for each plant taken. Some twenty-one wild plants are specially protected, and it is not permitted even to pick them.

'Well, can I still weed my garden and dig out wild plants?' people ask the Council for Nature, who produce a most interesting information sheet on the Conservation of Wild Creatures and Plants Act 1975. The answer to that one is that the Act does not prohibit digging up plants on your own ground. Cut wild flower collections (for children at flower shows, for example) are still permissible so long as they do not contain any of the listed plants, but they do tend to be frowned upon nowadays. At present we can still pick the majority of our wild flowers, though we should do so with discrimination.

This month our lanes abound in moonpennies (ox-eye daisies), and long ripening grasses, which give a fresh country look to an arrangement with, perhaps, a few garden poppies and cornflowers added. It is unthinkable that our children, and their children following after, might at some time not be permitted to pick simple wild country things to bring happiness to a June day.

Flowers in June

From the garden: Heuchera rubescens, roses, campanula, escallonia, spiraea (astilbe), early lilies, foxgloves, delphiniums, centaurea, smilacina, stocks, lady's mantle (alchemilla), poppies, paeonies.

JULY

How the earth burns! Each pebble underfoot
Is as a living thing with power to wound . . . .
Pitiful heavens! What is this we view?
Tall trees, a river, pools, where swallows fly,
Thickets of oleander where doves coo,
Shades, deep as midnight, greenness for tired eyes.
Hark, how the light winds in the palm-tops sigh.
Oh this is rest. Oh this is paradise.

Wilfrid Scawen Blunt

July, with fields toast-brown, weeds growing fast, and gardening in a big sun hat. Pink hollyhocks stand sentry at the gate and showers of scarlet roses hang from white trellis and peep in at the windows. The pond is cool and attractive to iridescent dragonfly and thirsty bird, a happy place to spend a lazy afternoon. But no rest for me. This is a busy month, with fetes and flower shows and days spent in steamy tents and marquees, those brave bastions of the sudden summer storm.

I seem to be on the telephone all day, or away from home on other tasks, but once in a while the dog and I walk down the shady lane and all is cool and green and sun-dappled. A goat tethered by the riding school gets untethered and nibbles at the valerian outside the garden wall. This old-fashioned cottage garden plant, pink, red, or white, is something I like to use in any mixed summer flower decoration for its faded sunbonnet charm. The name is said to mean 'to be healthy', and long ago valerian was used as a medicine. It seeds absolutely everywhere, and the root I planted six years ago has established its offspring in all sorts of corners, even in cracks in the paving where it is unbelievable that they find any nourishment. Of all the flowers in the garden, including some fairly rare ones, it is often the valerian about which people ask 'Please can I have a bit?'

Ferns

Indoors, the ferns seem especially refreshing on a humid day. I grow a number, for they add their own special lightness to any grouping of houseplants at all times of year. My best loved is the maidenhair. When seen against the light, especially on sunny days, the tiny patterning of spores can be discerned on the underside of the airy fan-shaped leaves. Lots of baby plants can be raised from them if the fern can find some moist soil to drop them on, which is why youngsters sometimes appear unexpectedly among my other houseplants.

Ferns generally have appallingly difficult names, though I have a friend who impresses me no end by tripping them off her tongue at the drop of a query. The old common names are perhaps more fun, and I grow the bird's nest fern 67

(*Asplenium nidus*), the sword fern (*Pteris*), and the asparagus fern (*Asparagus plumosus*). In the garden I also have the hart's tongue fern (*Scolopendrium*) grown for its long, slender, tongue-like leaves.

I have found that ferns grow well indoors in a downstairs loo window which never gets any sun, in north and east-facing windows, and windows shaded by trees. Positions on a room divider and in a hearth (in summer) seem ideal. Ferns must never be allowed to dry out, and as they enjoy a certain amount of moisture in the air mine seem to like conditions in the kitchen and bathroom too. I give them an occasional spray all over with an old liquid dispenser which I fill with tap water.

Outdoors and in, ferns have certainly made a comeback in recent years, though they have not yet regained the height of popularity they enjoyed in Victorian times. People then had special 'fern cases', like miniature indoor greenhouses, and 'fern bricks' were built into house walls to accommodate them. Ladies then, as now, enjoyed frilly green ferns in their windows and used them in their flower arrangements, particularly liking them in glass and silver epergnes. They also wore them demurely to fill in low-cut dresses and in their hair, as well as carrying them to parties and balls in beribboned posies. Gentlemen wore them with their buttonholes, keeping them fresh in tiny containers hidden behind the lapel. Many a fern was pressed in a book, for making into pictures and for using in winter arrangements. I find ferns can be pressed by ironing them on both sides with a hot iron (thought it does smell a bit!). With care they will then last many years for arranging, and for out of the ordinary colours they can be sprayed with car body paint, which, by the way, will preserve a fresh frond instantly. Spray both sides.

Rich pink hollyhocks by the garden gate provide excellent material for big, outside designs.

Shells stuck together with 'Polyfilla' make an attractive container for pink roses and grey leaves.

White and green designs

In hot weather, or even in cool rainy weather for that matter, white and green flowers and crisp green leaves are refreshing and always eye-catching. For a quick and effective table decoration I like to float a single white rose and its buds and leaves in a dish or shallow bowl of crystal clear water. When I first visited Windsor, many years ago, I bought a book from an antique shop which has delighted me ever since. Called *Twelve White Flowers*, and published in 1888, it features serene white flowers which anyone might still grow. Included are frosty white double camellias for spring, the descriptively-named pheasant's eye (or poet's eye) narcissus, marguerites, lily of the valley, white roses (I cannot do better than recommend the gorgeous Iceberg for its long untroubled flowering season), white sweet peas, clematis, azaleas, and Christmas roses (hellebores).

The book is an inspiration in July, when fresh green and white flower arrangements are always so very pleasing and there are plenty of white flowers in the garden. Frost-white campanula makes good outline material for large arrangements as well as being beautiful in the borders, and I pick white lilies, white pinks, white pansies, white snapdragon, white clematis, white chrysanthemums, white delphinium, and white mock orange blossom. I enjoyed white astilbe for many years until a summer drought took it from me.

To arrange calm green foliage with all these white flowers – or just on its own – is no problem, and green and white schemes are perennially popular for flower arrangement competitions. Choose the greens for their variety of form and texture. Popular just now are pointed hosta and griselinia sprays, round-ribbed bergenia (elephant's ear), prickly mahonia, and feathery evergreen thuja. But different effects can be achieved using white flowers with grey leaves, bronze, or gold. And why not green *flowers* as well? *Alchemilla mollis*, the flower arrangers' joy, and the green gladiolus 'Green Woodpecker', the strange green rose 'Viridiflora', green zinnias, and tobacco plant (*Nicotiana affinis* 'Lime Green'). Then there are the lace-flowered herbs fennel and angelica, the white-tinged green *Astrantia major*, and a shrub which I have down by the pond called *Bupleurum fruticosum*. It has invaluable green-yellow flowers.

White decor again

It was once the 'in' thing to have an all-white decor. Made fashionable by Syrie Maugham, wife of Somerset Maugham, the innovation was to have everything in the house white – walls, curtains, rugs, furniture – and white flowers in white containers unadulterated by green. She often favoured white enamel camellias in white china vases and gave parties at which only white foods were served! Perhaps she went a little too far.

Textured white walls and smooth white paintwork are popular again today, making the perfect foil for all flowers and leaves, plants, pictures, ornaments, books and furnishings. White reflects other colours in a room and really never 69

does appear stark or cold. Wallpaper with a large pattern can so easily spoil a flower design, giving a confused 'busy' background, though small patterns, oddly enough, can often trick the eye into a feeling that there is a quiet plain backing.

Texture, too, can be enhancing, and I for one always try to think of plants and flowers as part of the whole interior scheme. A friend of mine has her hallway lined with a pale almond-green hessian and finds it a perfect backing for arrangements in almost every colour.

Sweet peas

Summer to me just wouldn't be the same without the range of tender colours from the sweet peas. You can arrange them formally or, better still, informally in lavish bowlsful all round the house. Their perfume and charm are always welcome, always loved. The really old-fashioned sweet peas, with their extra-strong perfumes and bright colours can be grown from seed too, although the flowers are smaller than the more up-to-the-moment kinds. Sweet peas should be picked every day, and this is a pleasant task.

Lilies

With the sweet peas cut and arranged, I take a daily walk to see the martagon lilies, now in flower in purple and in white, and the tiger lilies. In my experience the best way to grow lilies is in tubs, where they make lovely garden ornaments and seem already 'arranged'. As cut flowers, they will fill a room with their scent and I love the perfume, but some people find it too heavy. Lilies are always admired for show work, however, and indeed they are very lovely, eye-catching, and somehow 'special', in spite of the brown or gold pollen which so easily comes off to stain petals, hands, and clothes. A good tip when taking lilies to a show, or to church for a wedding decoration, is to gently pack the centre of each bloom with cotton wool, so keeping the pollen away from the petals. Remove the cotton wool when you have finished handling the flowers, and just before judging begins.

Shrubs and grey plants

I like to grow shrubs as standards so that smaller things can be grown underneath and thus save space. I encourage many shrubs this way, including hollies, olearia (the daisy bush), *Garrya elliptica* (the winter catkin), among others. Just remove the lower branches neatly and make an uncluttered stem.

A frosty-grey shrub I would somehow manage to grow even if I had no garden (well clipped, it can be at home in a tub, a window box, or when young even a hanging basket) is *Senecio laxifolius*. It will 'take' easily from a cutting. All mine come from a bunch I bought at a Red Cross sale many years ago. The foliage is ever-grey, and both in the garden and in a flower arrangement the leaves are a foil to other colours. It has its best show-off period, when it throws a

70

This cool-looking garden border has a collection of foliage invaluable to the flower arranger, including hostas, euonymus and golden-flowered senecio.

display of golden daisy-like blooms; these emerge from sprays of silvery buds, which I particularly treasure.

Another cool grey plant, this time for the front of the border or for a decorative box, is *Anthemis cupaniana*, which for months on end supplies the house with innocent-eyed white daisy flowers. Cut the plant back after flowering and it will begin to flower all over again.

Showing a flower arrangement

If we take part in a flower arrangement show this month we may be able to use all garden flowers. But so often when we want particular flowers for a special arrangement they are over by the time they are needed. Some things, such as gladioli, paeonies, roses, carnations, and chrysanthemums can be held in bud for a few days by wrapping them firmly in newspaper then leaving them on the cool concrete floor of the garage until the day before they are required. Re-cut the stem ends and give deep pre-arrangement drinks in warm water.

THE FLOWER ARRANGER'S YEAR

Ten tips

When doing an arrangement for a show remember to:

★ Read the schedule carefully and conform to it exactly.

★ Condition your plant material well.

★ Make sure the mechanics of the arrangement are firm.

★ Be sure the plant material is more prominent than the container, accessories, background, drapes, etc.

★ Check that the plant material is in superb condition, with no broken petals or twigs or insect bites, though 'specimen' show blooms are not obligatory even at a specialist show.

★ Choose plant material which is in scale with the size of the container and the space allowed for the arrangement.

★ Keep the outline of your design airy but 'well-tailored' in shape, and aim for a well-balanced and uncluttered look using pointed shapes to lead the eye into the heart of the design.

Roses integrate perfectly with the rosy trails on the cushions and the chair's strong pink colour.

★ Ensure a good strong-looking 'heart' of the design by keeping a few bold, plain leaves and larger flowers for the important area at the centre front; all stems should seem to radiate from this 'heart'.

★ See that the colours of all the components of the design, including accessories, are well integrated.

★ Handle the flowers as little as possible, always holding them by their stems.

Cuttings this month

Summer heat means constant attention to watering the indoor plants and keeping a daily eye on the hanging baskets, which will sometimes require a soaking twice a day. If you like to water them *in situ*, a shower cap pulled on the underside of the basket can be a blessing!

Take cuttings from favourite geraniums and fuchsias this month. Cut straight across, just under a leaf joint. Remove lower leaves. Dip the stem ends in rooting powder and plant the cuttings round the edge of a pot filled with compost.

Lots of houseplants can be raised from cuttings or by division now. One of my best beloveds is the streptocarpus, with its long, slightly furry, and very soft tongue-like leaves, above which the orchid-like flowers of white, pink, rose, and lavender rise in drifts of colour on nice long stems – very carefree for cutting. We can grow them from seed, and I am told there are some super new colours coming along which will be introduced during the next few years. My current favourite plant is the colour of Parma violets and was grown from a leaf given me by a friend. I just pressed the cut end into a pot of soil. It all seems miraculous when one sees it for the first time, but many plants can be increased from a leaf, including African violets, and cacti and succulents. Simply plant the bottom of the leaf in compost. For *Begonia rex* start off a few new plants by standing leaf stems in small bottles of water.

Wild grasses

The lane, after a sudden summer storm has swept up the valley, becomes wet, steamy, and African-jungly. 'Good growing weather', they say. The dog and I venture out for our walk as the lane begins to dry up and though they are perhaps too wet for preserving I search the hedgerows for a few of the wild flowering grasses. We bring them home with buttercups and yellow toadflax to arrange in a brown saltglaze Toby jug which has been in the family for generations. Old Toby has always been used to hold arrangements of summer grasses for as long as anyone can remember so I like to continue the tradition.

Today's flower arrangers not only gather wild grasses but actually cultivate others in the garden, planting the seed of various decorative kinds in spring for gathering about now – preferably on dry days! Hare's tail, squirrel tail, Job's tears, blue meadow, fox tail, and other equally imaginatively-named grasses can be grown; if gathered when they are at absolute perfection they can be hung up 73

in small bunches to dry off in an airy room or shed. I don't usually bother with that – I arrange straight into old Toby.

A weeping pear

Most of us share our boundary hedges, fences, or walls with a neighbouring house, and it is good if we can co-operate with the people next door when it comes to planting things for our mutual advantage. Some things do clash, and I was slightly put out years ago when a carefully-planned colour scheme of muted lavender, magenta, grey, and cream in a border was marred by a bright orange rose spray which suddenly reared its head over the hedge! I got over the problem by planting a silver-leafed weeping pear (*Pyrus salicifolia pendula*).

This pear is such an appealing tree, attractive for a very long season. It has neat white blossom in spring and lots of glossy green doll's-house-size pears in early autumn. Beverley Nichols, I recall, has it weeping over a small pool. It is a very good choice for a small garden, but if you decide to buy one, do go to the nursery and choose your own. Mine has turned out to be rather stubby-topped and difficult to train into a graceful shape, though I prune out any over-enthusiastic branches each season to keep it small in stature. Growing under it I have pastel-coloured roses and campanula, while a 'Nellie Moser' clematis takes more colour up into the branches.

I have a good collection of campanulas, and over the years as they have increased they have become quite a feature of the garden in July. I specially recommend 'Loddon Anna' for its good rounded growth pattern in soft lilac-pink, and also the unusual white or blue-purple *Campanula latifolia macrantha*. The only fault I find with the campanulas is that I lack the time to go round each week cutting off the unattractive, individual deadheads.

Preserving roses

While roses are at their greatest peak do preserve one or two for your winter flower pieces. Use one of the drying agents such as silica gel, as described in the month of May, page 50. Alternatively, roses and stems of the delicious garden pinks and other sturdy double flowers can be instantly preserved by spraying them over completely with two or more coats of car body paint from an aerosol can. I like a number of lightly applied coats of more than one colour. Don't be heavy-handed. If the spraying is done well, and the colours carefully chosen, you get the effect of delicate porcelain flowers.

This is a pleasant task for July, while flowers are abundant and the long days move on, and August is suddenly upon us . . . .

Flowers in July

From the garden: Sweet peas, sweet rocket, lilies, dictamnus (burning bush), privet flowers, marigolds, snapdragons, petunias, and other annuals and biennials, hosta flowers, zenobia, acanthus, phlox and hardy geraniums.

74

AUGUST

Rich music breathes in summer's every sound;
And in her harmony of varied greens,
Woods, meadows, hedgerows, cornfields, all around
Much beauty intervenes,
Filling with harmony the ear and eye
While o'er the mingling scenes
Far spreads the laughing sky . . .

John Clare

August and the holidays, with cool wind-whipped seas washing up shells, bladderwrack, and shore crabs. Back home again in the garden, this is a month of lettuces in such numbers that I can think of making them into delectable pale pod-green soup. Border phlox, with their warm peppery smell, look joyous in the borders. Everyone's hydrangeas are a picture, and fiery orange berries flame the mountain ash trees along the lane.

But August is a funny month, in most gardens anyway – a betwixt and between time. The first roses are over really, and the second crop dallies in tight green bud. One perfect bloom for a bud vase is probably all that the roses offer, so it may be a good thing that I don't usually have time to arrange a bouncy bowlful.

Dahlias

Dahlias are the big drama of August, creating splendid impact in my borders. Without them there would be a between-the-seasons-sale effect, with the campanulas, delphiniums, and oriental poppies all cut down and nothing strongly cheerful to take their place. I try to plan for August, growing many things, such as petunias, stocks, zinnias, snapdragons and nasturtiums, as well as sweet peas, phlox, and montbretia, and various kinds of hydrangea, and I move pots of flowering plants around to fill in any 'dead' spots.

But back to the dahlias. I know that many people are not attracted to them, which is a pity. Perhaps they think only of the mop-head kinds associated with public parks. Yet there are so many sorts of dahlias, from dear little low-growing ones small enough for a window box or to edge a border, to the big and showy varieties. There are singles and doubles, anemone-flowered, cactus-flowered, pompon, water lily, and star-flowered, all of them in a great rich tapestry of colours.

I am sure there must be a dahlia to suit everyone. They will flower away 75

August

strongly from now until the first frosts, a truly remarkable feat from something which begins life as an oddly shaped brown tuber. It is interesting, I think, that along with many favourite arrangers' flowers they were introduced to this country by women. The Marchioness of Bute sent the first plants from Madrid to Kew in 1798. These died out, but more were sent home from Madrid in 1804 by another enthusiast, Lady Holland.

Dahlias last excellently in water whether picked in bud or when the flower is newly opened, and they are useful for arranging because of their roundness of shape, either on their own with a few leaves or as the main flowers in a larger design. I arrange them straight into warm water.

Scents of the month

Sweet peas, stock, and lavender scent the month. I have lavender close to the sitting areas in the garden, but sheer joy to me is a thick hedge of it outside a house in a small country town I sometimes visit. The bees and butterflies go mad with delight in it.

Nowadays I think the best way to enjoy the scent of lavender, apart from in the garden, is in a lavender-bag, pillow, or cushion. People never seem to be too sure about the best time to gather lavender for this purpose and for making into pot-pourri. In fact, the best moment is when the flowers have just opened, for

76 *Rosebay willow herb grows in profusion on a common – a good cut flower.*

A few stems of rosebay willow herb, arranged with golden filipendula.

Lavender is a delight in the garden, for flower arrangements, and to add to herb pillows and bowls of pot-pourri. Pick it when it is at perfection.

then they are at their most highly scented. They must be gathered in dry weather, as indeed must anything needed for pot-pourri. Hang up small bunches to dry, then strip away the flowers by running your fingers firmly down each stalk 'against the grain', and finally nip off the top immature bit of bloom.

There are a number of different sorts of lavender, by the way, apart from the old English, associated with cottage gardens. There is a deep purple called 'Twickle Purple', and pink forms and white, as well as one with a square-shaped flowerhead.

Lavender I think is lovely for flower arranging. I often use it with heather sprays to sketch in the outline shape of a summer arrangement; as both heather and lavender are pointed they are ideal for this purpose. The design is filled in with rounder-shaped and half open flowers such as border pinks, phlox, and roses, plus foliage, and the result can be very pretty.

77

A friend's hanging arrangement for a marquee at a wedding where the bride was marrying into an Irish family. Four small plastic-film-covered Oasis blocks were fixed to a flat board, using wire, to hold the stems of single daisy chrysanthemums, hebe, box and clematis seedheads: Design by Pat Mann.

Border pinks

One of everybody's favourite summer flowers is surely the floppy sweet-scented border pink. Some of those I like, which you might also, are: 'Freckles' (rosy pink freckled with scarlet); 'Cherry Ripe' (a light cheerful cherry colour); 'Daphne' (a single pink with a dark and swarthy eye); 'Inchmery' (palest pink, with a real old-fashioned scent); 'London Poppet' (white which is flushed with

78

pink and laced with ruby); 'Show Aristocrat' (soft pink with a buff eye), and 'Swan Lake' (white).

Herbs

A pleasant little task for a sunny day is to gather the harvest from the herb garden. I wait until the plants are dry and bunch them in my hand, tying them firmly with ribbon – usually bright post-box red or butcher's apron blue – and then hang them on the ribbons from hooks in the kitchen ceiling to dry. Actually, I leave them there all the time; they make a novel and attractive kitchen decoration and they are always ready to hand for flavouring soups and other dishes.

Herbs are useful and often lovely in flower arrangements. I remember a Press party at which the editor hostess had made a table decoration entirely of large leaf-green mint. Many people asked for a root of the mint, and it made a big talking point at the party. Had the journalists known it, they could have taken sprigs of mint from the decoration and 'struck' them into new plants. Mint quickly forms roots if left in a jar of water for a week or so. Then it can be planted in the garden, though as it 'runs about' I contain it in an old plastic bowl sunk into the ground.

Rosemary

I still have in the garden a very fine bush of rosemary, grown from a cutting given to me years ago by the lady of the manor at a garden fete after I had admired the old blue-flowered bushes growing as a low hedge round a terrace. We talked of how in the past it used to be carried at weddings, having been dipped in scented water and sometimes gilded.

Once, for a wedding where the bride's chosen flowers were to be of yellow, I used long sprays of gilded rosemary to give height and width to the outline of a very large pedestal arrangement which stood at the altar. The chancel lights and the altar candles lit up the soft gleam of the gilded rosemary between the pale yellow of the flowers.

Borage

Visiting the garden of a friend at this time of year in order to see her collection of very unusual plants, we paused for a fruit cup drink and I was enchanted to see that along with the lemon and cucumber slices she had floated in it a few flowers of blue borage, the herb of gladness. Both flowers and leaves of this herb have for centuries been used in salads and drinks. I have an old book which tells that 'the leaves and floures of Borrage put into wine make man and woman glad and merry, driving away all sadness, dullnesse, and melancholie'.

Buffet flowers

I came across a nice idea for table decoration when I went with a party of 79

journalists to visit four Midlands gardens and to partake of a sumptuous Victorian picnic to be served on a rural bit of green somewhere. Because of the wetness of the day we were instead invited into the ballroom of the house at Batsford Aboretum which is not normally open to the public. Here a buffet table had been made even more attractive by the addition of flowers, not placed in studied arrangements but used in a very natural-looking way to accompany each dish. A short-stemmed cluster of yellow daisy chrysanthemums had been arranged out of water to caress the side of one of the hand-raised pork pies, emphasising the brownness of its crust. White daisies with yellow centres were positioned among dishes made from fresh raspberries, greengages, and so on. The effect was lovely and I confess it's an idea I have since used for parties.

Houseplants on holiday

I suppose everyone who keeps houseplants is worried about what to do with them when going away on holiday. I plunge many of my houseplants out of doors in shady spots into the borders, pot and all, and with a flew slug pellets. Those which are permanently planted in self-watering pots are no trouble at all, and can be left indoors. I believe these gadgets will become more and more popular. Other plants can be left with a piece of bandage or lampwick connecting them to a bowl of water (one end of the bandage in the water, the other in the soil of the pot). Water moves along by capillary action, and the soil never dries out. A variant of this idea is to place layers of newspaper in the kitchen sink, stand bricks upon it and the plant pots on top of the bricks. (The pots must be clay, not plastic.) Water almost covers the bricks, and again capillary action does the rest. There are also capillary mats to stand in the sink, but a tap must be left dripping. Incidentally, I prefer the kitchen sink for this purpose rather than the bath – sinks are usually in a lighter position. I find that plants treated this way keep their good colour for up to two weeks and they don't go 'leggy'.

Another very good and simple method is to water each plant and put it right inside a plastic bag large enough to accommodate it without the leaves being pressed to the sides. Tie the top firmly, trying to trap as much air as possible inside the bag so that it makes a sort of balloon. Inside this mini-greenhouse, plants will do well for some weeks in a light position.

Indoor plants outdoors

Even when I'm not away many of my treasured indoor plants enjoy a little holiday of their own out of doors during the warm months. I just slip their own pots into the larger garden urns and so on and fill up the spaces between with clean gravel, peat, or one of the soil-less composts. Succulents in particular love to bask the days away in a sunny spot. They look extremely handsome on the wide treads of garden steps or on top of a low wall, where they give a
Mediterranean touch.

A suitable base will often integrate the flowers with an accessory. Here the line of the foliage and flowers is also accentuated by the sweep of the deckchair.

Pewter containers

A flowing orange-berried pyracantha touching the low eaves of the cottage makes my mother's garden look lovely just now. This is an excellent plant for a house wall. It has white flowers and, being evergreen, always looks smart. The flowers, by the way, are beloved by bees in the spring, and the berries are superb for picking and arranging with apricot-coloured dahlias, orange-red 'Super Star' roses, or anything with a warm tan or peach colour. I get out copper and brass containers for these arrangements, but pewter is also effective.

Pewter, to my mind and eye, adds a look of quiet quality to any flowers, leaves, or berries arranged in it. I like to use trails and sprays of grape-purple berberis fruits with the purple-leaf vine (*Vitis purpurea*) and seasonable fruits such as ripe figs, peaches, apricots, and little green grapes. The other day I enjoyed doing an arrangement in an antique polished wood tea caddy, with a tin hidden in it to hold the water. I used purple and pink annual salvias, the mahogany leaves of *Sedum atropurpureum*, and sprays of dark plum and fuchsia-coloured clematis.

81

August

Drieds

Gather the flowerheads of helichrysum (everlasting flowers) – the stems are hardly worth saving – and statice on dry days as they come to perfection, and put the helichrysum heads on wire cake-cooling trays to dry. The statice hangs in bunches. Helichrysum should be gathered before the centres show. They may be provided with 'stalks' made of a hook of florist's wire pushed right through the flower centres and then disguised with florist's tape in brown or

Paper poppies made by my friend Joan Patrick, with beautifully preserved achillea and delphinium.

82

green. A friend of mine wires them up and enjoys them drying out in her dining-room window in jars; they look like something in an oriental bazaar.

Anaphalis is often grown by flower arrangers for its small, pearly, off-white flowers, which dry easily on the plant. In fact, they never seem anything but dry even when they are newly emerged young blossoms! The stems will dry rigid if the whole thing is hung up immediately after picking. I was given samples of anaphalis, commercially dried and coloured in Italy, by the director of a firm in Surrey which imports such things for flower arrangers. There were 28 colours, from palest apricot, through yellows, greens, and blues, to browns and pinks. You can achieve similar effects at home by using water dyes in which you stand the fresh picked stems, although I find it easier to spray lightly with proprietary car body paints.

Pressing flowers

Broken down into small posies, anaphalis can be used to make dried flower pictures, calendars, and so on. Indeed so can many small flowers, buds, tendrils, and leaves throughout the year, if they are pressed in a flower press. You can buy a small press for this purpose or make your own with a couple of pieces of hardboard, some blotting paper, and a suitable weight such as an old-fashioned flat iron or a brick. Pick your plant material when it is in good fresh condition and place it carefully between sheets of blotting paper, positioning some flowers so that they will press as open blooms, others to show their profiles. Put a piece of hardboard either side of the blotting paper, place your brick or other weight on top of the 'sandwich', and leave until the flowers are flat and crisp to the touch. Remove and store in boxes in a warm, dry place. Other suitable subjects for pressing are pansies, forget-me-nots, nasturtiums, godetia and lastly delphiniums.

Seaside material for flower arranging

August is still very much a holiday month, certainly for those with children at school. I like a day out to my nearest bit of the coast whenever I can manage it during the summer to go beachcombing for things to use in my flower arrangements. Flower arrangers see a world of possibilities in things which other people would pass by without a second glance. Textured pebbles, stones, and shells are useful mainly for covering pinholders. The beach at Budleigh Salterton is renowned among arrangers for the beauty and variety of its pebbles, and at St Ives I always pick up some of the flat, black stones which shine like jet under water when used with flowers in a low dish. I am told you can find real jet on the shoreline at Whitby, and fascinating pieces of driftwood can with luck be found on any beach, but with so many flower arrangers around nowadays you have to be lucky to get a really good find. For those holidaying inland, woods (especially old coppiced ones) may prove more fruitful.

In flower arranging terms, driftwood is any piece of wood which has been 83

naturally weathered by the elements. You don't have to search for it if you have neither the time nor the inclination, for you can buy it. One hot August day I drove down a valley in Cornwall to meet a couple who made it a full-time job to tour the coasts and countryside, all over Britain, looking for driftwood, which they brought home, dried out, cleaned, and sometimes shaped, ready for sale. If you prefer to find your own, it can be scrubbed in detergent, bleached in household bleach, stained, varnished, or turned grey by soaking it in water with plenty of salt.

'Seascapes'

One way of displaying seashore bits and pieces is to compose a 'seascape', grouping a number of objects together with suitable flowers and leaves, fresh or dried. My flower club had a class in its summer show one year called 'I do like to be beside the seaside', and arrangers had used not only driftwood but beach towels, bits of deckchair canvas, sand, shells, buckets and spades, pebbles, and starfish. Plant material, which for a show must always predominate over other items in an arrangement, included the thistly grey foliage of eryngium, blue hydrangea, tawny and gold-coloured daisy chrysanthemums, dahlias, and maram grass. Before arranging fresh hydrangea, by the way, submerge the whole flowerhead in water for an hour.

Speaking of competitive flower arranging, many people get a bit worried over what they may use as plant material in an exhibit with a nautical or seaside theme. Driftwood, cactus skeletons from holidays abroad, and twisted sun-baked British or foreign seaweed all come under the blanket term of plant material, and may be included in most arrangements unless the schedule specifies 'fresh plant material only'. Shells, pieces of fretted sea-fan (sold in many seaside shops), coral, feathers, stones, pebbles, and figurines are obviously non-plant material. They may be included in classes where accessories are allowed.

Berries

The mountain ash by the garage already hangs with thick clusters of its orange-red berries, so that gathering a few for an arrangement on the kitchen window ledge makes it seem more like autumn than August. But autumn still seems a long way away, and first we have the lovely time poised between summer and autumn . . . September.

Flowers in August

From the garden: Hydrangea, hollyhocks, lavender, annual poppies, eryngium (sea holly), tree lavatera (L. olbia), cephalaria (giant yellow scabious), crinum powellii, catananche (Cupid's love dart), biennial clary (Salvia sclarea), achillia, cornflowers, Helichrysum and other 'everlasting' annuals, begin to gather for drying.

SEPTEMBER

Season of mists and mellow fruitfulness,
Close bosom-friend of the maturing sun;
Conspiring with him how to load and bless
With fruit the vines that round the thatch-eaves run;
To bend with apples the moss'd cottage-trees,
And fill all fruit with ripeness to the core;
To swell the gourd, and plump the hazel shells
With a sweet kernel; to set budding more
And still more, later flowers for the bees,
Until they think warm days will never cease . . .

John Keats

Here's a month which gives that opulent golden feeling very special to late summer. When buff-pink button mushrooms push up overnight through the wet grass in the park, and blackberry gatherers in straggly family groups work their way up the hedgerow on the other side of the lane. Thistledown drifts as the day warms up, and hips, haws, plums, and apples ripen in the sunshine.

Seedheads and dried flowers

As the faded summer borders are tidied up for the end of the season I like to retain a few well-shaped seedheads, keeping them tucked away in a dry place for winter decoration, using them in their natural colours or else lightly bronzed, gilded, or spray-painted at Christmas. Candytuft, sunflower, foxglove, campanula, poppy, gladiolus, Japanese lantern, and many more are splendid providers of material that has dried out naturally on the plant. 'I would never have thought of using spent hollyhock seedheads in a flower arrangement,' remarked a laughing friend when I rescued a little bunch of these half-ripe green-buff seedheads from her garden rubbish heap. Arranging them in a colour scheme of cream, nasturtium, soft red coral, lime green, and tan, using dahlias, tobacco plant blooms, snapdragon, roses, and strawberry leaves turning colour, we agreed they look most pleasant, and my friend went back to rescue a few for herself!

Flower arrangers cut and use many items of plant material which are not actually flowers or even flower-like. Often these cannot be called pretty in the accepted sense – toadstools, for example, sweet corn sheaths, gourds, and such – handsome, striking, dramatic, yes, but not really pretty. It's a matter of developing an imaginative eye, ever on the lookout for shape, character, colour, texture, in any natural material, and ideas for interplaying them in an arrangement.

85

Leaves are often as beautiful as flowers. Here a mix of blue, tan, grey and green includes various conifers and fronds of Royal Fern (Osmunda regalis).

Now is the moment to look out some of the things we have been preserving during the summer, and in the coming weeks and months enjoy them in arrangements all over the house. We can build up whole designs – of splendid size, if we like – using nothing but dried material, or else mixing dried material with fresh flowers for really eye-catching effects. Try using, for example, an interesting seedhead or a cluster of home-dried flowers stuck in beside the plant in its pot to give it added height and visual interest, or to provide colour when its own flowers have faded. Some very interesting surprise effects can be gained this way.

The hydrangeas are almost at the perfect state for preserving; catch them as their flowers (or, more correctly, bracts) begin to feel like suede rather than silk to the touch. I dry them off quickly in jugs of water on top of a boiler or radiator. They will last for years – something worth remembering if you do not have a hydrangea in the garden but are given a few flowerheads. If and when, in time, they lose colour they can be sprayed with spray paint. Any tints and shades in the blue-green range are attractive and realistic. People have actually con-gratulated me on the way some of mine have 'kept their colour'!

The *Sedum spectabile,* so popular this month with the butterflies and bees, dries off to a good tan-brown head. This stands the winter well, giving a glow of warmth to a bare place. It is a first-class plant for tubs and outside garden urns, again winning very special marks for looking just as good in the 'off' months if the seedheads are left *in situ.* It looks specially attractive on a cold winter's day when it is lightly frosted.

Using preserved material

Any subjects we are growing for winter decoration should possibly be picked this month as they come to perfection. Don't leave it all too late or they will stand the risk of spoiling by wind and wet. Pampas grass should be gathered just before each plume expands, and it will open nicely indoors. It is best of all if you preserve it in glycerine, when it will stay light and silky for years rather than turning winter-dusty and brittle. Bulrushes for preserving should also be picked on the side of immaturity. For more about how to preserve see page 150 under Preserving.

Very attractive swags, drops, and garlands can be made for unusual wall and table decorations using many of the preserved things we have been squirreling together through the season cones and other seedheads, flowers, bracts and leaves. Shells can be wired with fine florist's wire to thick cord or stuck carefully in a pattern on a length of coloured linen-covered card or directly on to a strip of finely sanded wood. Don't get carried away and be tempted to use too great a variety of plant material just because it is all so lovely and you have gone to the bother of preserving it. Try to create a well-balanced and effective design with a clear, forceful colour scheme. For Christmas wall hangings, bits and bobs painted with metallic paints look splendid among natural colours on a scarlet felt background. In all these forms of decoration, aim for a good repeat pattern, with planned areas of interest appearing regularly through the design. This has a way of appealing to the eye rather better than an informal mix.

Lighting flower arrangements

As the days grow shorter, lighting becomes more important. How we place our lights indoors can influence the visual effectiveness of our houseplants and flower arrangements. Spotlights, for instance, can be exciting on a bold clean-cut arrangement, though they can, if badly placed, create shadows and a feeling of gloom which destroys the charm of smaller flowers and leaves. Wall lamps and candlelight, too, can have a disturbing effect on an arrangement, changing its intended appearance by casting shadows, but shaded table and standard lamps close to the flowers cause fewer difficulties. Most artificial lights change the colour of flowers and leaves to some extent. Some dark reds can seem almost black, a delicate blue may become wishy-washy, but clear pinks, cream, orange, and yellow all sing; well-lit white simply sparkles – points worth bearing in mind if you have to buy flowers for, say, a dinner party.

September

The importance of leaves

Almost all flowers, no matter how beautiful, need leaves to show them off really well, and flower arrangers often say that they would always grow foliage plants even if they had no room in the garden for flowers – because flowers can always be bought but leaves are rarely for sale in florists' shops. And attractive arrangements can be achieved using nothing but leaves of one kind or another.

As we all know, many leaves flush, stain, streak, or stipple with new colour as they die. Up and down the borders paeony and azalea, *Amelanchier canadensis* (snowy mespilus) and many other plants and shrubs are positively flaring and crackling in a sudden fireworks display, so that the borders are as fine a sight as in many a famous arboretum. But it is not for long, so I seize the moment to include these autumn leaves in my arrangements.

Chosen for colour

Better and more lasting value can be found in things which grow with an inbuilt permanent leaf colour, blue, grey, emerald, crimson, cinnamon, ruby, bronze, etc. Any flowers are really an extra bonus. They include plants easy to find in many nurseries nowadays, including *Rhus cotinus* (*Cotinus coggyria*), many conifers, a large number of heathers (calluna), hebes, eucalypts, ivies, hollies, ornamental cabbages and kales, periwinkles (vincas), and phormiums (New Zealand flax).

From a list which could be as long as your arm I must find room just to mention *Atriplex halimus* (a silver shrub), annual ruby chard (which has brilliant scarlet stems through the winter), epimedium, *Berberis thunbergii atropurpurea* (a plum-maroon colour), *Berberis thunbergii* 'Rose Glow', semper-vivum (houseleeks), *Cyclamen hederaefolium* (various cream marblings on green), *Rosa rubrifolia* (pinky-purple), *Philadelphus coronarius* 'Aureus', golden privet, *Lonicera nitida* 'Baggesen's Gold', *Hebe armstrongii* (invaluable khaki-gold evergreen), *Hosta fortunei* 'Aurea' (soft yellow), *Hosta fortunei* 'Albopicta' (marbled in gay primrose, green, and gold, slowly turns green as the year advances) and *Hosta sieboldiana* (with blue-grey paddle-shaped leaves).

But half the pleasure of gardening for flower arranging is choosing and discovering for yourself. So ring up a friend, get out the car, or catch the bus, and away to your nearest plant nursery.

September berries

September comes in spiced with a glad profusion of handsome berries and fruits. They arrive in such variety that when I gather a bunch for the house the effect as they lie on the kitchen work top has something of the look of circus trappings, with stars, globes, beads, buttons and whirls in showy, racy colours. A shrub called *Callicarpa rubella* for instance, has hundreds of tiny surprising bead-like fruits of light purple. These will last all winter in the house. I gather the stems then strip away the leaves to expose the fruiting clusters.

Top left: Virginian pokeweed (Phytolacca americana) *is a handsome herbaceous plant with fruits like purple berries (poisonous).*

Top right: Arum Italicum pictum *is a very 'pickable' plant. It has marbled arrow-shaped leaves, interesting flowers, and these ripening seedheads.*

Left: The cheerful starry flowers of a late summer beauty, hypericum (Elstead variety) turn to desirable nail-varnish-bright fruits.

High in the orchard a snowberry (*Symphoricarpos rivularis* 'Constance Spry') is weighed down this month under heavily berried sprays of white, which will be carried by the shrub in most winters until February. I enjoy arranging these later sprays with winter bulb flowers or with Christmas roses (hellebores) or white silk roses and at other times with white dahlias and real white roses.

'Red-ink plant'

'Whatever is that?' people ask as they turn the corner into my secret garden and get their first sight of the 'red-ink plant'. Its real name is *Phytolacca americana*, and it is also known as the Virginian poke weed, and as pigeon berry. A herbaceous perennial, it dies right down in the winter and comes up again the 89

following year. Just now mine is at its most striking; its magnificent spiky branching heads are set all summer long with sticks of pink-green flowers, slowly turning into pale green then purple-pink berries like particularly beautiful blackberries. It is much favoured for flower arrangement and certainly has a very long period of beauty from its early summer creamy-pink flower stage (when the young lime-green berry clusters begin to form in the centre of each flower), right through to mid-autumn, when the whole spike has coloured to a fantastic sight – a close mass of dark wine-purple fruit. Because of its poisonous properties it is wise to keep this plant out of the way of children and pets, and to wash your hands after picking or arranging it.

Further along our secret garden is a raised border whose pride is a small shrub which has other more unbelievable-looking fruits; this time they are turquoise set off by an outer star of dull ruby red. If you fancy this the name to remember, and order from the nurseryman, is *Clerodendrum trichotomum*. Not quite so unusual, but still rather off-beat, is *Ilex crenata*, which is a holly with black berries as a change from the familiar red.

Fruits and seedpods

Other fruits around this month (as well as the windfall apples the foxes are eating in the orchard) include those of cydonia, which should now properly be called chaenomeles. Gather a few and put them into a tiny basket or a dish and they will scent a warm room with a soft fragrance which is really very pleasant. Cydonia is closely related to the quince, but the true quince is equally to be sought for. No matter how small your garden, it makes a tree or shrub with a long period of interest. First, big flowers like pale pink apple blossoms deck the tree. These are followed by large pear-shaped golden fruits which hang on until quite late in the season and always set me humming to myself 'I had a little nut tree, nothing would it bear, but a silver nutmeg and a golden pear'. I'm afraid you don't get the silver nutmegs, but then you can't have everything, can you? Quince blossoms and fruits are good for arranging but you can also put a little of the fruit into apple pies.

Iris foetidissima (also known as stinking Gladwyn and roast beef iris) carries its funny smudgy coloured flowers, to which no-one but a flower arranger would give a second glance, in summer. It saves up its grand surprises for the autumn and winter days when the buff-green seedpods ripen and split open (cut the stems just before the pods pop open and allow them to burst in the warmth of the house). Inside each one there are hidden seeds neatly set in rows like coral beads. With care (a spot of hair lacquer sprayed on is helpful) the seed sprays will last indoors all winter, and they are a fine sight arranged in copper, pewter, or brass containers. I always leave some on the plant for welcome colour in the dead of winter, however. The name roast beef plant refers to the imagined scent of the cut stems and bruised leaves.

Nowadays many flower arrangers grow roses not merely for their flowers but

A September crop of John Downie crab apples. Even a young tree bears so well that it is a pleasure to heap the fruits like beautiful jewels.

also (and in some cases mainly) for the magnificent autumn hips which some of the shrub roses produce. One such highly to be desired rose is *Rosa moyesii* 'Sealing Wax', with vivid cerise single blooms on long arching wands but memorable in late summer for its mass of fiery pitcher-shaped hips.

September

Flower arranging clubs

September, some people might think, is the end of the flower arranging season. In fact, the very opposite is the case and flower arranging clubs and evening school classes on the hobby are now settling in for their autumn and winter programmes. Certainly this is a very good time to join a flower arrangement club. Most are affiliated to the National Association of Flower Arrangement Societies, and generally meet every month, some in the evenings and some in the afternoons. The one I belong to has some 300 members, others are quite small, but all follow the same sort of pleasing pattern.

Usually at each meeting there is a talk and demonstration by a qualified demonstrator, there are sales tables and plant stalls, perhaps a raffle to help raise funds, and generally a flower arranging competition which everyone can enter if they wish; many clubs split the monthly competition into sections for novices and more experienced arrangers. At my club we have a very successful sales table and another where members can sell plants they have raised, home-made jams, flower containers they no longer want, and so on, with the club taking a commission of 25 per cent for its funds, and some members being regularly able to augment their incomes in a small way.

A couple of times a year like most clubs we have a show open to the public to view – ours are usually spring/summer, and Christmas – and these are in aid of some good cause. We are often involved in bigger shows too, at area and national levels, and in such pleasures as flower festivals in cathedrals, churches, and stately homes. Once or twice we have even arranged flowers for royal occasions. But, above all, flower arrangement clubs are great makers of friends.

There are today over 1,000 clubs with a total membership in the region of 100,000: local public libraries usually have details of those in the area close to home. For anyone just starting this delightful and absorbing hobby there are classes in most areas nowadays, run by the evening institutes and adult education centres, with experienced flower arrangers as teachers. You can study what you will, traditional and modern styles, Ikebana – the Japanese art of flower arranging – Christmas arrangements, church work, and so forth.

The National Association of Flower Arrangement Societies publishes its own excellent magazine, *The Flower Arranger*. All these things are very worthwhile as the basis for what can be a lifetime's interest . . . and with one thing and another they can get us happily through to October!

Flowers in September

From the garden: Dahlias, scabious, the second flush of roses, sunflowers, gladioli, *cynara* (globe artichoke), chrysanthemums, *amaranthus* (love-lies-bleeding), golden rod, *cimicifuga* (bugbane), red hot pokers, *crocosmia* (giant montbretia), *lathrus* (everlasting sweat pea).

OCTOBER

Now stir the fire, and close the shutters fast,
Let fall the curtains, wheel the sofa round,
And, while the bubbling and loud-hissing urn
Throws up a steamy column, and the cups
That cheer but not inebriate wait on each,
So let us welcome peaceful evening in.
William Cowper

Mornings come in crisp and fresh like new-picked October apples, each slightly different from the next. Brightly plumed pheasants are glimpsed as they scuttle away when Sue the dog explores along the edge of the field. Afternoons turn chilly, we put back the clocks, and country walks ankle-deep in damp leaves turn into expeditions to gather driftwood, berries, dock, fungi, and Queen Anne's Lace 'skeletons'. But it is good to get home to tea by the fire.

Tidying up the borders ready for the winter brings a feeling of calm and peace to the garden, and to me. How well the foliage plants stand out, clean-cut against the newly-forked earth. Over the years I have worked to give each cottagey border a new face for every season, and so the autumn appearance is just as pleasing as the summer view. As in a well-constructed flower arrangement, every item is meant to add something to the overall design.

Before the frosts come we should think about bringing tender geraniums (pelargoniums) in from the open garden, along with any begonias, and fuchsias which are not of the hardy kinds, or we will lose them with the frost. When we take the geraniums out of the ground it is staggering to see the amount of growth they have made, and it may be a problem to accommodate them until next year. Yet new plants cost such a lot of money. It is too late now to take cuttings, but both geraniums and fuchsias can have their roots severely cut back to fit them into small pots, as long as the top growth is cut back hard too, so that only stumps of a few inches are left. Keep them in the window of a cool but frost-free room.

If you have a conservatory or similar extension it is worth considering installing a heater of some kind to use in the frosty weather. You can then bring into it annuals still growing well in pots and tubs, such as snapdragons, petunias and lobelia. Continue feeding and watering them and they will continue flowering for ages. If sunrooms and conservatories are kept warm, instead of left as winter store-places and junkrooms, they can be full of interest, and pleasant places for meals or enjoying a hobby among growing plants. Even an unheated sunroom, greenhouse, or glass porch can provide flowers, such as tubs of American spray perpetual-flowering carnations, for much of the year.

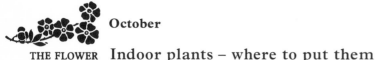

Indoor plants – where to put them

For anyone without a greenhouse or glazed porch, pot plants are the thing, but before buying a new plant stop a moment and think where you are going to put it. From now on, the light in even the lightest room is generally poor from a plant's point of view, and usually the more colourful flowering plants need positions at least in a really good window light. Subjects grown for their green leaves, on the other hand, will put up with a rather darker situation further into the room.

Some pot plants are intended only as fairly temporary decorations like a bunch of cut flowers, but if you do want something longer-lasting, and like a change from geraniums or pot chrysanthemums, a fairy primula (*Primula malacoides*) is always pleasant. I like to make a collection of these small primulas, buying perhaps one a week for some weeks and then planting them together in a big flower container. They are specially pretty when planted up with fresh green ferns and trailing tradescantia.

The average home has many darkish corners where a green growing plant is specially desirable as a decoration. And it is interesting that green potted plants are even grown on North Sea oil rigs as aids to relaxation and to reduce stress. Small pieces of furniture, shelves in alcoves, etc, will make suitable homes for collections of chosen plants in leak-proof pots. In modern houses, or older properties which have had two rooms knocked into one, an open-shelved room divider full of a trailing curtain of green growing plants is always a fine sight, and occasional flowering plants can be added for a day or two before being put back into a better light.

Another good idea is to have a room partially divided by a long white plastic plant trough, or a group of the largest-sized square white plastic planters pushed close together, and filled with jungles of tall-growing and climbing subjects. White plastic trellis brings a summer garden look to, say, a flat which has no proper garden, and you can get a similar effect with long bamboo poles. Carpets are sometimes rolled round these for delivery and some carpet shops give them away.

But don't limit plants to the sitting room and dining room. Plants will provide a lovely welcome in the hall, giving the nervous guest something to discuss as she takes off her coat! The loo is another place to site a tall green plant, and the bathroom and kitchen, with their sometimes steamy atmospheres, are perfect for many plants which would naturally relish tropical rain forest conditions. I once grew a superb honey-dropping wax plant (*Hoya carnosa*) in my bedroom window, close to the bed, and as a poor sleeper I appreciated its soft nocturnal scent.

Plants for medium light

There are many plants with striking foliage which like average home conditions. The peperomias, for example, are happy in a medium light.

Bromeliads, with their rosette-shaped foliage, will put up with a dim light, though if they are to flower they should get some dappled sunlight. The aspidistra, long back in fashion with flower arrangers (its leaves are treasured as cut plant material), will grow almost anywhere except in a sunny window. Dieffenbachias, which have splashed charteuse-green, cream, or white markings, will flourish well in filtered shade but they need warmth and humidity.

When geraniums (pelargoniums) are brought in for the winter they are a useful bonus for an arrangement. Here Oasis is wired to the warming pan.   95

Pot-et-fleur

Stripy or marbled dracaenas, ivies, kangaroo vines (*Cissus antarctica*), philo-
dendrons, and glossy green ficus, all have different leaf patterns and add impact
to a room, especially when a number are grouped together as in a flower
arrangement, where shapes and colours are played off against each other.
Coloured foliage plants I can recommend, which have just as much appeal as
flowers, are coleus, *Saxifraga sarmentosa* (the strawberry saxifrage), and croton,
all special favourites of mine. Cut flowers can be added to a group of plants in
one container if you snuggle a little jar, a well pinholder or a plastic toothbrush
holder down among the plants to hold water for the flowers. Such a design, if it
includes no extra cut leaves, is called a pot-et-fleur in the flower arranging world.

Green plants

Some superb green foliage plants can become an immediate feature indoors.
Groups of them look particularly handsome in large copper or brass containers
backed perhaps by a brass tray or a Victorian lamp. For cool semi-light
situations I specially recommend *Rhoicissus rhomboidea* which is a good climber
with glossy evergreen leaves; cascading plectranthus (a very easy one for
beginners); and the little creeping helxine, or baby's tears, one of the few plants
I know which must always have its feet in water. Incidentally, there are green,
gold, and silver foliaged helxines, and if you want to be really economical you
can buy a pot of helxine and split the plant with a friend.

One green plant pleases me specially because I grew it from a stem given me
by a friend after a flower arrangement show. It is the moisture-loving umbrella
plant (*Cyperus alternifolius*). If you know someone who has this plant growing
well she will probably give you a stem complete with its radiating green top like
an umbrella's ribs. All you do is pop the stem, upside down, into a bottle of
water. Miraculously after a few weeks it will push down roots from the centre of
the leaves and can then be planted in a pot of compost as the new growth begins
to shoot around the old stem. This can then be cut off and thrown away. The
thing obliges in this way because it is a waterside plant from Madagascar and if
any of its stems get broken they drop head first into the water and push down a
few roots, so spreading the colony. It makes a good subject for cutting, too.

Garden flowers

I have carried in from the garden some close-to-opening white-budded sprays
of the beautiful devastating weed, convolvulus. I am trying so hard to eliminate
it from the garden, but in the meantime I feel I might enjoy its flowers indoors,
and arrange them with their own delicately spiralling leaf sprays. The flowers
arrange pleasantly with green and white variegated geranium leaves from a
houseplant, in a white china Victorian vase shaped like a hand holding a shell. I
suppose that if these were rare flowers, instead of weeds, we would treasure
them dearly.

Gladioli in a container made from part of a car silencer covered with wallpaper. The container is by Bernadette Wright.

Silk flowers arranged in a glass container deceive the eye into thinking them real, more so if real foliage is added.

Small clusters of little pink *Cyclamen neapolitanum* continue flowering in the dewy grass under the robinia (false acacia) tree halfway up the lawn. Each flower, with flyaway petals typical of all cyclamen, is like a ballet dancer pirouetting on one leg, though it measures only about half an inch on its four-inch stem. In colour, these tiny yet perfectly hardy cyclamen can be anything from white to deep pink. The attractively dappled leaves, with their purple-pink undersides, make equally good cut plant material which lasts excellently in water. I arrange them, as if growing, in a small shallow dish with a few sprigs of an autumn-flowering double pink heather which gives extra height.

The deep rich blue autumn gentian (*Gentiana sino-ornata*) is in flower in lime-free gardens. It is sometimes seen for sale in bunches as a cut flower, making an excellent and exciting buy. You can arrange it in a bunched cluster, 97

which is very spectacular, or split the bunch and add the flowers to arrangements of other small blooms.

It is surprising to find the pink nerines as florists' cut flowers, and growing in the garden, so late in the year as this. They look altogether too frail to be blooming among wet leaves and autumn mists. The bulbs came originally from

These attractive mock flowers are made of wood shavings. Made-up flowers are allowed for competition if made completely of natural plant material.

98

South Africa and the bowdenii group is hardy but in the majority of gardens does best when planted in a sunny border under a warm wall. Each stem goes up to about two feet with a little posy at the top, of pale pink or soft red lily-like flowers. When in bloom nerines will still withstand a slight frost, and as cut flowers they last well, with unopened buds continuing to open in water. Remove individual flowers as they go over.

October leaves

In a local park I pick up pale lemon-gold fan-shaped leaves of ginkgo (the maidenhair tree) which make a thick carpet on the ground, and leaves of the scarlet oak (*Quercus coccinea*) for pressing. From the garden I bring in leaves of the beautiful rough-textured vine, *vitis Coignetiae*, suffused with gold and crimson and peach, for arranging fresh, while a purple vine which I grow, *Vitis vinifera* 'Purpurea', now has a special bloom on its claret-red foliage and whether pressed or used fresh, nicely accompanies last flowers from the purple, lilac and pale green 'cup and saucer' vine, *Cobaea scandens*. Another delight is the *Cotinus coggygria* foliage now turning yellow and soft tints and shades of pink, to accompany pink or yellow groups of cut flowers and fruits. Bergenia leaves if grown in dry situations often turn lovely colours at this time of year. *Bergenia cordifolia*, for example, has the typical leathery leaves, some of which may now well be turning a brilliant lacquered crimson and gold.

Clematis for planting

My 'golden' arch, planted with golden ivies, has a fine clematis at its very best in the cool autumn air. This is C. 'Jackmanii superba', very effective against the rich yellow and green glossy leaves of that other good garden plant, the ivy called 'Paddy's Price', prince among ivies. If you live in or near a chalk area where the wild clematis – or traveller's joy – grows you can carefully disentangle long trails of it to preserve in glycerine. Don't leave the seedheads too long, for the moment they begin to 'fluff' they won't take up the glycerine. The leaves are attractive, and they too will preserve well either alone or in the sprays. If you have to do church flowers on winter days you will find that lightly gilded preserved wild clematis sprays are ideal for making low sweeping outlines. The stems will not mind going in water with fresh flowers for up to a week or so. To keep them longer in water the stem ends would have to be varnished to prevent mildew.

I believe everyone loves a clematis in the garden, and there are many different ones available. Some people are now growing them over the ground on a few short pea-sticks or some wire netting, so that the mass of bloom looks up at you. As for the ones which are grown up walls, even the most house-minded husband cannot complain that clematis will cause damage for they cling not by aerial roots or suckers to the brickwork but by tiny twisting tendrils to, say, a bit of plastic-covered mesh.

99

Clematis for cutting

Now let us have a look at some of the most beautiful, for all make good cut flowers. Clematis 'Blue Diamond' is a love with sky-blue flowers and white stamens; it blooms for a long time, from June to September. 'Daniel Deronda', a semi-double with violet-blue early flowers, is a June-to-October winner. (Oddly, the later flowers are singles.) 'Duchess of Edinburgh' is double white with ethereal green-white flowers and I do rather rave about a small-blooming specie clematis called *C. macropetala* 'Maidwell Hall' which has soft lavender-purple flowers overlaid with grey; the hanging bells in May look like bright little moths as they climb the winter-flowering *Garrya elliptica* which grows at the front of the house.

Pressing Virginia creeper

I have a theory that people specially like the time of year at which they were born. My birthday month is October, and I have always specially loved the month and its flowers. For my first birthday party, I'm told, my mother decorated the table with trails of autumn-coloured Virginia creeper. (These leaves will last out of water for a few hours if given a long drink first.) Nowadays I like to preserve a few leaves for use in the winter; they can be ironed on both sides with a fairly hot iron. Keep them flat for a week or so inside a heavy book.

Autumn arrangements

For a flower arrangement as part of the decor of a party after dark, anything which shines and glows is an added attraction. Use shiny containers, and place the arrangement near a lamp. For a drinks table, arrange the flowers in a candlecup fixed in the neck of an empty green or brown glass wine bottle, with lighted candles to match the flowers. A decanter filled with coloured water and a candlecup, used as a container, will catch the light in festive fashion. Candles seem appropriate to any flower arrangement at this time of year, when the dark evenings are upon us. And you can light the candle or not, as you please.

A useful gadget you can buy is called an Oasis Frog; made of plastic, it is designed to hold Oasis water-retaining foam steady in a container. I use a couple of them stuck together with Oasis Fix to hold a candle in an arrangement; one pronged end sticks into the foam and the other grips the candle. The foam does not break up, and the candle stands steady. Even complex designs using four or five candles can be achieved by using a number of 'frogs', or one can sticky-tape four cocktail sticks to the base of each candle.

Florists' flowers which come in sprays on short individual stems make excellent buys for table arrangements. Chrysanthemums, freesias, and carnations, for example, will be available now. If we grow geraniums in a tub these too will give us odd snippets of both colourful foliage and glowing flowers at this time. Cutting back the bushy plants can be a positive advantage, in fact, if space is a problem.

I am always greatly cheered to see at this time of year that Nature is already laying up the promise of spring. Every year it surprises me afresh to see how early infant catkins are plumping up on the hazels down the lane, promising fat buds form on the garden rhododendrons, and I can pick an October posy of polyanthus and scented viburnum if I fancy, as a taste of things to come.

Garden flowers including gladioli, dahlias, helichrysum, sedum, and sprays of atriplex hortensis cupreata (an annual), arranged informally in a textured plastic wastepaper bin; unusual use of a patterned container. 101

October

The true flowers of October, though, must surely be the border chrysan-themums. In many colours, some shaggy, some daisy-like, some like little globes, they always please me, particularly as they last so delightfully long as cut flowers. Scrape and slice open the stem ends and they will go on for weeks. I never disbud mine because I like the sprays of smaller flowers which are the result of letting the plant go its own way.

For early flowers next year, sweet peas can be sown in October in three-and-a-half-inch (9 cm) pots. I leave mine in a cold frame all winter with the top off except in the hardest weather. You could use an unheated greenhouse, certainly to germinate them, but the plants should not be coddled. Regular watering is necessary, and an occasional treatment with liquid slug-killer, plus some mouse bait put down if you have mice in the garden, for both slugs and mice will find your sweet peas a scrumptious winter delicacy.

Your first show

If you enjoy arranging flowers why not try your hand at a show arrangement? Autumn shows are in full swing just now, or you can join your local flower arrangement club and have a go there. Certainly there is no better way of improving your skill with flowers for the home than entering a show from time to time. The first thing to do is get hold of the show schedule and study it, reading all the rules and the details of the various classes. See whether the classes are to be judged by an accredited judge of the National Association of Flower Arrangement Societies and according to their Schedule Definitions, as detailed in a booklet you should be able to get from the club or show secretary or direct from NAFAS at 21a, Denbigh Street, London SW1V 2HF, price 10p at time of going to press.

In deciding which class to enter, don't get carried away; it is best to enter one or at most two. If the class has a descriptive title, remember that your design must try to interpret and live up to the title. It's a good idea to get your plant material, containers, and so on, together some time before the show day and have a trial run at home. Whatever the class, keep the design crisp, try to produce a neat, shapely outline, and work up a good colour harmony with all the components.

On the great day, get to the show in plenty of time so as not to be fussed. Win, or lose, gracefully! And spare a thought for the judge. Like all NAFAS national judges who go to shows the year round, I often have to be up at six in the morning to get to a show on time, and may not be home again much before six in the evening. And there are many shows in November . . .

Flowers in October

From the garden: *Helenium, schizostylis,* chrysanthemums, *Gentiana sino-ornata,* Chinese lanterns nerines, nasturtiums, hydrangeas, colchicum, garden heathers, liriope (like grape hyacinths).

NOVEMBER

The day becomes more solemn and serene
When noon is past – there is a harmony
In autumn, and a lustre in its sky,
Which through the summer is not heard or seen,
As if it could not be, as if it had not been!
Percy Bysshe Shelley

This is the very eve of winter, with leaves like small brightly-coloured birds whirling past the windows and smoke from garden bonfires drifting across the valley. Mornings are clear with forget-me-not blue skies or else pearl-grey and drizzling and the bare hedges drip, and every walk is an adventure in the mist. Familiar gateposts and trees loom like strangers, and the last blackberries are cold and tasteless on the tongue. Like an ancient never-quite-completed piece of needlework, the fading year is gently being folded up – but already winter jasmine and laurustinus flowers are out and the buds are swelling nicely on the camellias.

Along the field path, dew-dripping rose hips are silhouetted against the autumn backdrop of mist, yellow, orange, and flame. But a wild shrub to make you stop in your tracks if you come upon it unexpectedly in November has berries in a colour scheme that somehow suggests some very mad hedgerow goings-on. Shocking-pink lobed fruits split open to expose orange-coloured seeds clustered inside. This sizzler goes under the old name of spindle (real name, *Euonymus europaeus*), and though it is worth watching out for in the countryside I wouldn't actually grow one in the garden, because they are the winter host to blackfly which in the spring will go directly to the broad beans! The hard wood of the spindle used to make the spindles of spinning wheels and such things as laundry pegs, knitting needles, skewers, and toothpicks. If you come across spindle berries try using them in arrangements with bits and pieces gathered from the garden, as a useful exercise in 'risky' colour schemes.

Chrysanthemums

Out of doors and indoors too, chrysanthemums have an acrid, earthy, pungent scent which is so very much a part of autumnal flower arranging. All daisy flowers are easy on the eye to most people, and the single daisy chrysanthemums now come in so many subtle colourings that they should fit with all home colour schemes. The flowers are effective when arranged with roses, and the berries of viburnum and firethorn (pyracantha), and the coloured leaves of autumn to tone. Such an arrangement in an old brown kitchen jug gives me much pleasure. 103

November

A secondary placement of matching flowers and a few rosy apples, arranged in a well pinholder at the jug's foot, adds interest to the lower part of the design; a slice of smooth brown wood as a base links everything happily together. But autumn does not have to be all oranges and tawny shades if these do not happen to suit your colour scheme.

Double chrysanthemums, particularly those very large mop-headed affairs, are a slight embarrassment to many women when they get a handsome present of such a bunch, or whose husbands grow them so enthusiastically, the bigger the better! Take a few such mopheads, cut their stalks down slightly to give different heights, and impale them on a pinholder placed in a heavy bowl-container. There these proudly proferred blooms will show off their charms with great spirit and aplomb. Make them look as important as possible with the addition of strong colourful garden leaves, and display them in a prominent 'show off' manner for all to admire. The home grower will usually not thank you for cutting the thick stems down overmuch, and sometimes then the only thing to do is to cluster the great heads on their long stems as given, using something very sturdy, such as a large stone garden urn, as a container.

Arranging very simply in moss-covered chicken wire, to give the effect of flowers growing from the container, can be another very effective method of displaying the bigger-bloomed chrysanthemums. Other garden flowers available, or leaves, can be included with their stems cut shorter to give added depth, and therefore interest, to the design.

Seedheads for a sculptural effect

In the wild if you are lucky you may come upon hogweed (cow parsnip) seed skeletons. The stems of the giant hogweed can go up to ten feet tall, topped with huge seedheads – ideal for pedestal-sized arrangements. From my garden the strong upward-thrusting lines of the celery-flavoured herb called lovage catch my eye. I have not previously thought of using this plant in flower arrangement – only as a culinary aid. However, following a whim I gather two of its long thick stems and produce a modern-looking decoration for the hall. By this time of year the stems are tough to cut and I use a sharp kitchen knife. I carefully remove all seed sprays, dead leaves, and the side shoots which grow in an alternating way up the stems, so creating a pattern of slanting cuts. The effect of the material when arranged indoors seems strangely foreign and exotic. The hollow white-centred stems are green and ridged like watered silk and are well set off by thick handsome lines of pale donkey-brown banding at each stem division.

I choose a low modern dish container of rough texture and brown colour to display the two stems together on a pinholder. Bringing in three dried-out green-brown runner beans, I add these too, impaling them on to the pinholder as if they were something rare and expensive from abroad. As the lovage stems slowly dry out and naturally preserve themselves over the coming weeks they

*Create atmosphere by designing around   called for the muted colourings of coral,
a favourite picture. This seascape   driftwood, and dried plant material.*

should make an effective sculptural setting for an ever-changing variation of
flowers from chrysanthemums to scarlet florists' carnations.

Using thick stems decoratively

Thick stems, by the way, are always eagerly pounced upon by those flower
arrangers keen to attempt modern and abstract work. Sometimes pieces are cut
out of the stems to make non-realistic decorative patterns and outlines,
sometimes thinner stems are bent and pinned to take on new shapes, sometimes
stems are cut up into varying lengths and reassembled in strange eye-catching
original ways – their appearance altered, perhaps by being stuck sideways all the
way up other vertical stems. Not everyone finds such advanced designing
particularly appealing, but equally strange things sometimes happen in nature.
Onion stems can go to seed and take on weird unreal-looking curves and bends.
Hollow stems sometimes bend back on themselves. Branches and flower stems
will naturally fasciate – that is, grow in an odd, flattened or contorted way.
Modern interiors can take such designs for they will often act as a link with
rough-textured furnishings, blond woods, and 'masculine' colour schemes.   105

'Art deco' arrangements

It is amusing now that the nights are drawing in to make a brightly-coloured art deco flower arrangement, so typical of the Twenties and Thirties. We can use autumn flowers, berries and leaves, either fresh or preserved, in any of the clear sparkling cheerful colours which were all the rage at that time, such as tango (a burnt orange named after the popular dance), emerald green, violet, cerise, all the clear strong blues, cream, and even silver and black. Art deco vases, bowls, and parts of teasets typical of the period between the wars are now very much the 'in' thing. Typical shapes in china and glass have a distinctive and often geometric Odeon Theatre or Hollywood look, decorated with such things as sunbursts, boldly formalised flowers, and bright, cheerful, outgoing colours. The art deco look was inspired by all the flamboyant colours (called Eastern colour) and exciting movement of Diaghilev's Russian ballets. To arrange in these containers choose bold clean-cut confident plant material in good strong colours.

Not all containers of the period show the same exuberant use of pure colour, and in homes where the mock Tudor style of interior was preferred such items as brass jugs, earthy pottery pitchers, pewter, and china flower rings and troughs (to hold little mixed flower collections) were favoured. The fashion was invariably for one sort of flower or perhaps two, closely massed together and usually with no additional cut foliage, which gave the flowers added impact of colour. Alternatively, flowers were arranged in an informally free and airy manner, with little in the way of 'mechanics' being used other than glass 'roses' (circular glass stem holders) or 'wire nets' (caps of stiff wire mesh). Although Constance Spry's books on flower arranging first burst upon the world in the Thirties the majority of homes were not much influenced by her style until much later. It is interesting to collect flower arranging books of the period by such authors as Menie Watt and Anne Lamplugh for ideas to copy such as the 'floating bowls' – round, low, pottery or glass bowls in which bright flowerheads were floated around china birds or figures of diaphanously-clad ladies. These figures are nowadays very collectable. Indeed, many of us may have art deco containers tucked away in cupboard or attic and we can look on them now with a fresh eye to their flower arranging possibilities.

Flowers to buy

With plentiful summer flowers now over, we begin to look around for things to arrange and may well turn to the florist, finding with a bit of a shock how small a stock of fresh blooms is to be seen at this time of year. As customers we are tending to buy fewer flowers for ourselves, and perhaps the flower shops are suffering. Still, this is the month when anyone who loves flowers might treat themselves to, say, a spray of out-of-season pinks or a bunch of South African nerines, a perfect rose for a bud vase, or a stem of spray chrysanthemums.

Preserved garden flowers, seedheads, and foliage can now be arranged in the

Even the curly window catch is part of this design, arranged in situ.

As flowers become scarce, silk daisies make a refreshing decoration.

blocks of dry foam sold for the purpose, and will bring pleasure all winter if they are rearranged from time to time. Cut the foam with a sharp knife to a size which fills the chosen container and extends an inch or so higher than the rim.

No-one who glances into a florist's shop nowadays can fail to have noticed that all kinds of artificial flowers are the 'in' thing. Made-up flowers created by country housewives in Italy are imported into Britain by the lorry-load. I found this out when I drove over to see one of the biggest importers of materials for flower arrangers. He told me some of these 'flowers' are made of wood shavings from the furniture industry in Florence. Though they may seem expensive to buy, they are a good investment. I have some which are ten inches across; the natural wood is slightly gilded and they are quite splendid enough for arrangements in the grandest settings. For a flower festival in an abbey church a friend and I used them for huge arrangements on either side of the ornate altar, along with lilies, fruits, foliage houseplants, and fresh leaves of bergenia and fatsia also lightly, airily part-sprayed with gold. I have other wooden flowers in various colours which I use all winter in homely arrangements. Occasional leaves which die and fall from a houseplant, such as grevillea, ficus, or aspidistra, can be used for months in a flower decoration.

Silk flowers
Silk flowers are beautiful in the extreme these days, and often very hard to distinguish from real ones. And if we change them as frequently as we would fresh flowers they make useful winter-day decorations. Plastic flowers were never as lovely. It is my boast that I once won £10 in a competition – part of a 107

big show at Olympia – for spotting the two plastic flowers which had been added to a very large display garden of real blooms. From a distance of ten feet, too!

I have liked silk flowers ever since I used to wear pretty hats, for weddings and flower shows, decorated with full-blown French silk roses. Today the silk blossoms available on long plastic-covered wire stems really are a delight, a treat. You can buy not only sprays of tight rosebuds but also sweet peas, fuchsias (I use these among my winter fuchsia plants), paeonies, carnations, daisies, and many more. Silk roses come often in subtly distinctive colours that no real rose has ever assumed. Some people resist all mock flowers and fruits, but I find silk flowers very acceptable, lovely things in their own right. Arranged with fresh or preserved material, they have a very grand air about them, especially at this time of year when it is marvellous to be handling an abundance of any 'out of season' flowers.

I must say I am particularly jubilant about mixing them with potted foliage plants so that friends walk into a room and are for a moment deceived into thinking that, say, my *Begonia rex* has produced a big round unconforming bloom or that the grevillea, with its dull bit of leafless stem at the bottom, has a miraculous glowing flower. Another bit of fun is to arrange silk flowers in a glass container, which tricks the eye into believing that the stems are in water.

'Hat' flowers
Slightly cheaper to buy than the best long-stemmed florists' silk flowers are the milliners' flowers sold for hat decoration. Mixed sprays and single blooms are

Casually grouped dyed real grasses accompany five stems of dried achillea. The stems of the grasses, too fine for a pinholder, are held in dry flower foam.

A basket holds two solanum (winter cherry) plants with an accompanying arrangement of clementines and mock berries.

available; I always take the mixed sprays gently to pieces so that I can rearrange them as I wish. The roses, I always think, look charming if 'floated' – dry, of course – across a shallow dish, or arranged in a small silver cream jug. The field and cottage garden flowers for hats include buttercups and daisies, cornflowers, poppies, and anemones, and they all look well, arranged in small baskets, or popped in among arrangements of fruits or real leaves so long as they don't touch water. Chicken wire can be used in the normal way to secure them. Mock flowers seem very acceptable as arrangements for parties, where they withstand hot and dry air and look gay and carefree, and as temporary decorations for office reception rooms, churches, and so on.

Plastic fruits

Though I hate plastic flowers, I think plastic fruits nowadays are marvellous. There are grapes, oranges, strawberries, apples, and pears, and the peaches in particular have a soft flock finish which is enormously attractive. I have a large collection of plastic grapes, and use them constantly in arrangements at home and elsewhere. Beware, however, using any mock flowers or fruits for competition work except perhaps in Christmas shows or if the show schedule specifically allows them.

Glass fruits and flowers were once popular. I have some glass strawberries and grapes, sadly now much chipped, which date from Victorian times. Very realistic glass tulips with curvy stems were sold in the Thirties, and I believe they were quite cheap at the time. Recently I saw a bunch of these for sale in an antique shop on the Isle of Wight for £50, and I wondered if today's plastic flowers will ever be such a price in years to come. Somehow, I don't think so.

Houseplant bargains

The seeker after a fresh potted houseplant will find that the shops are at their lowest ebb around this time of year, usually with nothing really colourful or interesting on offer. Naturally enough, the growers are trying to keep back as much stock as possible for the forthcoming Christmas trade, and plants begin to grow expensive as nights become cold, boilers are turned on, and the nurseryman's expenses rise. Bargains do crop up from time to time, however, so it is worth keeping an eye open. Potted azaleas and cyclamens, for example, are sometimes offered fairly cheaply during the early part of this month as – maddeningly, no doubt, for the grower – they come into bloom too early for Christmas and have to be sold off. Keep a look out on market stalls, but if the weather is very cold don't buy plants which have been exposed to the chill.

There is no reason in the world why, with care, houseplants bought now should not be kept going and nicely flowering over Christmas. Obviously, we must choose ones with plenty of fat buds and a fresh, crisp look about them – no brown or yellow leaves, no drooping or signs of wilting. Never buy a poorly-looking plant, no matter how low the price. Towards the end of this month and

the beginning of December, florists may be selling off poor examples of those striking Christmas goodies the poinsettias if, for instance, they have lost their lower leaves. These make a good buy, surprisingly perhaps, because you can use the brilliant 'flowers' in Christmas arrangements. Burn the cut stem ends, give a long drink, and they should last in an arrangement right over the festive season.

Plant now

The great pink, white, or red tropical-looking trumpet flowers of the amaryllis (hippeastrum) appear quickly after the boxed bulbs are planted. I have even known them to bloom within a month of planting, so if you start one off now you could get it to flower for Christmas. Try to select a bulb which is large and heavy, measuring two-and-a-half inches or more. The bulb may already be showing green shoots at the top when you get it, but this is all right so long as these are not damaged. Plant in an eight-inch (20 cm) pot with broken crock at the bottom for drainage, and use a good compost. Half the bulb should be above soil level when planted, and you need to leave a space between the soil surface and the rim of the pot to make watering easy.

Place your amaryllis in a sunny window, and bring it further into the room on cold nights. Remove spent blooms as they fade, to prevent the plant setting seeds, and when all flowering is done the bulb can be put outdoors next spring to ripen, if frosts are past. The plant needs to be fed and watered throughout the summer, and the bulb is then lifted in September, dried, and stored indoors before being started into growth again in November.

Marigolds

In the garden I can still pick odd flowers from the ordinary pot marigold (*Calendula officinalis*), and a cheerful marmalade-coloured pot of them stands outside on the terrace. All yellow flowers were once regarded as the special plants of the sun, and marigolds are ideal to take as a gift to someone who is not well or feeling low. I like to arrange them nice and easy in my old copper tankard, but they also look well in a yellow enamel kitchen milk jug. In an earlier age, before carpets were common, marigolds were much liked for strewing on the floors, along with rushes and sweet-smelling herbs; they must have looked very pretty. Beef broth was incomplete without a few dried marigold petals, and medicinally they were used to treat measles and varicose veins. The name calendula is an allusion to 'calendar' and the fact that the plant is in bloom through almost every month of the year. At one time these flowers were simply known as 'golds', but 'marigold' is in honour of the Virgin Mary and the legend that she wore this flower on the bosom of her gown. I don't know anyone who doesn't like this simple flower, and even a friend of mine who has no garden makes it his first choice for his window boxes. Certainly marigolds make very attractive pot plants for a balcony or sunroom, and they last a good long time as

cut flowers. They dry well too.

A favourite potted plant 'blooms' with surprise flowers – two spray chrysan- *themums cut down and arranged in a hidden container.*

Trends

The days of grand formal dinner and luncheon party flower arrangements at home are probably long gone, and today's party tables are rarely large enough for anything more than small informal arrangements anyway. With Christmas coming up, a simple design of pots of growing flowers, such as early cyclamen or 111

November

pot chrysanthemum, may be all the busy working woman has time to arrange. Small, modestly-bunched flowers look easy on the eye as a homely table decoration at any time, even for a party. There is something slightly embarrassing about being faced with an over-arranged not-a-stem-out-of-place dining table flower arrangement when you go out for a friendly meal. These don't somehow seem to fit in comfortably with today's informal nice-and-easy ways of entertaining. They are perhaps now 'old hat', what a young writer in *The Lady* magazine described as 'Those Aunt Agatha style arrangements which take hours to achieve'!

A number of matching containers for flowers can be made by spray-painting margarine tubs (I really don't have shares in the spray-on paint firms!), or using such things as empty date boxes. Simplicity is often a virtue, and perhaps one of the most economical forms of flower arranging is the Japanese way, called Ikebana, which I am sure you will find very soothing and appealing to the eye . . . and now can be a very good time to join a class in Ikebana, since the chrysanthemum is the national – and one of the favourite – flowers of the Japanese.

Fashions in all things come and go, and people often ask themselves where the next trends in flower arranging will take us. I have a feeling that there will be a greater move towards the simple and uncontrived, as well as a closer link-up with the classical flower art of the East. But we shall see.

November the Fifth

Meanwhile, I have to do an arrangement for a late Bonfire Night party. I use chrysanthemums, dahlias, and roses with vegetable and nuts, all arranged around a turnip lantern made by hollowing out a turnip and standing a nightlight inside. The arrangement is to stand under a shelf holding grinning golden grapefruit faces, made by removing all the fruit through a hole made in the back of each grapefruit then carving a face on the peel. These, I hope, will make an effective decoration for the conservatory at night. Outside, potatoes and chestnuts wrapped in silver foil will be roasted in the bonfire embers.

Suddenly, Christmas does not seem so very far away . . .

Flowers in November

From the garden: Snowberry, berberis, and pernettya in fruit, the last dahlias, roses, echinops, and other lingering border flowers, seedheads such as dictamnus, love-in-a-mist, candytuft etc.

From the shops: Chrysanthemums, roses, orchids, carnations, statice and other dried flowers.

DECEMBER

Some say, that ever 'gainst that season comes,
Wherein our Saviour's birth is celebrated,
The bird of dawning singeth all night long:
And then, they say, no spirit can walk abroad:
That nights are wholesome; then no planets strike,
No fairy takes, nor witch hath power to charm;
So hallow'd and so gracious is the time.

William Shakespeare

In town and village squares Christmas trees, calm Nativity scenes and 'the lights', are going up. Biting frost and the first sprinklings of snow bring ring dove and mistle thrush, woodpecker and wren, hungry to the bird table and in view of the house windows. Across the fields, the castle and the parish church are floodlit for Christmas. In town, flower shops burst overnight into a revelry of colour and the pleasant custom of hanging a garland on the front door is seen again. For this is the most magical month of the year.

As I take a last walk round the garden after working in London all day, a low palest orange sun flushes the breast of a late-feeding great tit so that for a moment I think it is an unfamiliar species. On the side of the hedge which the sun never reaches as we near the shortest day, the frost of one night lingers on to greet the frost of the next.

Early winter flowers
But this is usually the best month of all for the early winter flowers – the starry yellow jasmine, the shell-pink viburnum (*V. bodnantense* 'Dawn') by the garage wall, and the winter prunus between our house and next door. Yet it still seems early, somehow, to be picking these wintry things for the house. I rarely do so until Christmas, even then saving my main treat for Twelfth Night, when all the Christmas decorations come down. This is utterly illogical, of course, as by then the flowers may be slightly, or greatly, frost-bitten. Yet 'everything in its season' seems to be an inbuilt desire and most of us will really never get used to having a 'shop' chrysanthemum available all the year round when in our childhood they were connected only with crisp autumn and frosty winter days.

Christmas decoration
The faithful laurustinus (*Viburnum tinus*) becomes a quiet eye-catcher once again, making a comfortable backing for a couple of stone cherubs sporting 113

naked at the far end of the garden. In the same area a pert scarlet waterproof ribbon bow, large and important enough to be seen from as far away as the lane, festively decorates the big archway, with its covering of gold and green ivy. I love to make the garden a part of Christmas, and I rather envy the house next door, where the family put fairy lights over a handy fir tree in the front garden. You can see it twinkling seasonably across the fields on the darkening afternoons.

Even if you have no garden, no need to despair! Why not hang bunches of artificial fruits, a bow of waterproof ribbon, and some shining Christmas tree birds to decorate the clipped bay or box trees you might have standing either side of the front door or on your balcony in town? Last Christmas a friend made a smart pair of mock clipped-holly-ball trees to stand inside the two long, deep sash windows of her downstairs flat. She did this by embedding broom handles into two jumbo-sized plant pots of cement, with crumpled chicken wire on top to hold sprigs of variegated holly all cut the same length for a uniform effect. They were finished off with dramatic scarlet flock-ribbon bows to match the big pussy cat bow on her front door.

At least I shall have time to decorate some of the houseplants, as I always do, setting them all-of-a-show with glass, silk or flock Christmas tree ball decorations 'arranged' on foliage hidden sticks, like growing flowers, or with seasonably coloured ribbons.

One of the nicest things about flowers and plants is their ability to spread joy, and at this time of year small things bring pleasure. For town friends, with only a window box for a garden, a generous country bunch of perfect evergreens – long-stemmed holly, complete with berries if possible, ivy, fir, spruce, and gold-green elaeagnus – all tied up with a broad Christmas ribbon, makes a most welcome and imaginative gift in the weeks before Christmas.

I took a friend one of these bunches as a 'thank you' for having me to lunch. She has a big cherub-encrusted urn in her minute walled garden; in summer this spills a wealth of trailing geraniums but, to be frank, it does look a bit bleak when winter takes its bright summer loveliness away. Then it stands empty, forlorn, just waiting around. After lunch, just to please me I expect, she filled the urn with my evergreens, using a bit of chicken wire tied across the top, creating a fine bold arrangement with the ribbon bow at the front. It lasted well into February in her sheltered garden. 'Though the birds soon took all the holly berries,' she said. Which reminds me that I must warn you to gather your holly for decorating early in the month, before the birds descend and strip it of berries. Evergreens last well when cut and left outdoors now; I stick the cut ends into the soil at the edge of the vegetable garden and cover the whole thing over with old curtain nets to keep the birds away. When the decorations come down, on or before Twelfth Night, I give the birds the now dried-up berries in 'bird pudding' made by stirring together melted fat and a mix of crumbs, canary seed, cheese, and other tasty morsels.

A Christmas cactus should flower year after year in time for the festivities. This colour may be difficult in many homes, but others are to be found.

Winter posy

I like to make a posy for a Christmas guest's dressing table with sprays of jasmine and a few purple winter-flowering iris (*Iris stylosa*, or *unguicularis*), and the pale roses, faded now, that I may still be able to take from the garden, plus the first gathering from the Christmas rose (*Helleborus niger*). There are many stories about the Christmas rose but my favourite involves Eve, who sat weeping outside the gates of Paradise after the apple-eating affair. It was snowing, and no flowers bloomed. An angel sent to comfort her caught in his hands one of the descending snowflakes. Miraculously, it immediately turned into the first Christmas rose. So I add the miraculous flower to my posy.

Christmas shows

A flower show at this time of year? People sometimes find it hard to conceive 115

that there could be such a thing when flowers are not exactly at their most profuse. Yet most flower arranging clubs put on their major show of the year in the weeks just before Christmas, full of spectacle and sparkle. Though fresh plant material, traditional evergreens, seasonable flowers, 'frosted' fir cones, and the like, are always in evidence, man-made materials are usually allowed in Christmas show schedules, and arrangers go to endless lengths to interpret each class title. Sales tables at these shows are always good hunting grounds for the offbeat decoration.

How do you get ideas for such competitions, people often ask. Well, a class title such as 'Christmas round the fireside' could be interpreted by using fresh

116 *A welcome at the door: berries, evergreens and bows wired to a folded magazine.*

or dried plant materials in fiery oranges, flaming reds, and vigorous golds, with holly and other Christmas evergreens on an old iron fire trivet with a copper kettle 'singing' in the 'flames'. A few grey seedheads of old man's beard (preserved wild clematis) could be added to suggest wisps of ascending smoke, and a realistic china cat or some carol music spring to mind as the kind of things which might make suitable accessories. At home, the idea could be adapted for a hall table to make a point of interest when friends happen to come by for a Christmas drink.

You could, of course, interpret a title such as 'Christmas Eve' in a totally different way, with carol singer figurines, frosted evergreens, and skeletons of hedgeside weeds, or you might take up the theme of the babe at Bethlehem. One may have a suitable religious figure around which to construct an arrangement of fresh flowers, but a member of my flower club constructed a superb Madonna for a Christmas show, using a milk bottle with a ping pong ball in the neck for a head. Around it she draped a long blue 'cloak', taking it right over the top of the head. When the figure was placed in the arrangement, with its back to the viewer, it looked most effective and no-one suspected its simple beginnings. I admire people who won't be beaten by difficulties.

Garlands and swags

During the weeks before Christmas I look forward to seeing once again the Christmas garlands which appear each year on many of the fine Georgian doorways in the old town which lies snug in the valley across the fields. Sometimes this will be a simple bough of evergreen with a green or scarlet ribbon bow flying mightily in the wind, sometimes it is a circular design of rosy apples, cones, ivy, and fir. In the last few years I have noticed that Christmas garland making is really catching on and now spreads out as far as the recently erected housing estates circling the town, where many of the shiny new front doors are made brighter still with ribbon bow and holly.

There are various methods of making a Christmas door swag or garland. One of the easiest ways is to bind bits of evergreen, rose hips, lightly gilded fir cones, berries, and real or plastic fruits, with florists' reel wire or fuse wire, to a folded-up magazine, which makes a good firm base. The magazine is folded thinly lengthwise; at the bottom wire on a spray of evergreen, then bind on a second piece, and so on. Repeat from the top, working in interesting bits of other material in clusters as you go.

For a garland you could attach your plant material to a wire coat hanger which has been opened up and bent into a circle – this is a good old well-tried way. Last Christmas I made a most effective decoration for our panelled white front door, using a large square plastic mesh sink mat as base. I rolled the scarlet mat round on itself, corner to corner, to make a sort of funnel, wiring it to prevent it unrolling. On to this it was easy to fix evergreen thuga, berries, and long scarlet ribbons. (By the way you can buy waterproof ribbon from a florist.) 117

The pressed flowers and leaves of the year can be glued to cards and calendars. Turn upside down and tap gently to remove any loose bits. Starting from one corner, press clear adhesive plastic film on the card. (Designs: Beryl Clements.)

Dried arrangements

Most folk enjoy receiving a preserved flower arrangement as a Christmas present. Quick to make from larkspur, helichrysum, achillea, dyed grasses, statice, and bits of fresh conifer (which keep well out of water and stay a good colour for a long time as they dry out naturally), the design can be based directly on a piece of tree bark or white expanded polystyrene tile. Wire a small piece of flower arranging foam to the bark or tile to support the stems.

Landscape in snow

This is the children's special month, and for them it is an idea to make a Christmas snow scene if there is no actual snow. A white polystyrene tile makes a good cheap base, or a piece of ridged cardboard packing material, and on to this might go a well pinholder hidden by a couple of 'logs' – driftwood covered in sprayed-on 'snow'. But don't forget when spraying mock snow on to branches

for arrangements, a very light hand is needed. The arrangement itself, being held on the pinholder, could be of suitable tree-like twigs, seedheads, grasses, ivy, or whatever you might be able to find in the garden or growing wild, or some suitable preserved flowers might be added. Figures of birds, beasts, and so on add to the fun, and such touches as a mirror could suggest a frozen pond. Children love creating these frosty scenes.

The Tree

It's time to think about getting the Christmas tree. Only quite recently, the artificial tree in green, silver, gold, or white was all the rage, but now I am happy to see the traditional fresh real tree is 'in' again. Buy one with a good root system intact, if you can find one, plant it in a large pot of good compost, and keep it cool as you can and watered like the growing plant it is, and you may well be able to plant it in the garden after Christmas. Perhaps it is the faint scent of lavender about a real Christmas tree which makes it so special. My mother, who is proud of being a Victorian, recalls the ceiling-high trees of her childhood, set with real flaming candles which had to be carefully controlled with a damp cloth on a stick. Presumably because of the risk of fire, no present was wrapped in paper, so you could see the delectable wooden horse on wheels, the dolls, and the sugar-mouse and the jack-in-a-box hanging there in store for you.

It is amusing to have a tree decorated to a theme. A year or two ago I talked to the man in charge of window display designs at Liberty's in London, a store which always produces very original ideas. He told me that plans for Christmas are made in the previous January, and in that particular year they had worked to a Tudor theme, with each window having a huge natural Christmas tree hung with fruits, cones, pomanders and garlands of nuts. I thought how magical such a tree would look in any home which had a large entrance hall, spotlit after dark and glimpsed through a window from the dark cold street outside. 'Good display is pure theatre' declared the display manager – something a Christmas flower arranger could well remember, I think.

Every year real Christmas trees become more expensive, so perhaps there will be a revival of a much more ancient emblem one day, the old English kissing bunch or kissing bough. Made from a circlet of wire or osier (willow), covered close with evergreens such as box or rosemary, the beautiful kissing bunch was suspended by ribbons from the ceiling. It held little presents, sweets, and such decorations as shiny stars, perhaps home-made from tin, and paper rosettes. Always there was a ring of candles, secured at intervals round the circle, and below hung seven rosy red apples on scarlet or blue ribbons, and under all this was a bunch of mistletoe. My mother still remembers the beauty of these bunches from her Derbyshire country childhood. Some kissing bunches were intricate affairs, with more than one circle put together to form a globe or crown. The candles were always lit on Christmas Eve for a short time, on Christmas Day as the centrepiece of the festivities, and on each of the twelve days of Christmas. 119

December

Ideas for presents

There's still time to make some small presents – the kind of things which are a happy offshoot of flower arranging, trifling individual gifts which will please because of their originality and charm. All those bits of plant material we have been pressing and preserving through the year can be turned into place mats, pictures, calendars, cards, and we can make up our own herb filled cushions.

Inexpensive plastic picture frames may be bought from the big stores and it is easy to cover the backing provided (or the vividly coloured picture which may be in the frame) with a scrap of fabric smoothly glued on, or with a stick-on plastic which has a linen finish. Secure preserved flowers and leaves with touches of an adhesive such as 'Uhu' to form a pleasing arrangement. Such things as butterflies cut out from magazines and real snail shells can be added.

An idea of mine one Christmas was to use big wooden curtain rings as frames, to make miniature pictures representing each of the seasons. The plant material was arranged on rounds of card glued to the backs of the rings. But perhaps table mats are among the most acceptable of presents, though they necessitate having rounds or oblongs of glass cut specially. Cut strong cardboard pieces the same size as the glass, covering both sides with felt before doing your design of pressed flowers, buds, leaves, and so forth. Carefully place the glass over the arrangement and stick the edges firmly together with self-stick tape, finishing off with upholstery trimming – this gives a really luxurious effect.

Felt stockings to hang on the tree this year and such things as covered boxes of sweets are also on my list to be decorated with preserved flowers; indeed, members of my flower club make lots of the latter every year for elderly patients in a local hospital.

The New Year

And so, with Christmas here once again, we come almost to the close of the year with, however, a promising new one just about to slip in around the corner. It's a year which could be richer, livelier, altogether more sparkling than the last if each of us resolves to bring flowers further into our scheme of things. Just think of it – if every flower lover in the land determined to make sure there were always flowers, or a flowering potted plant, in a window that is seen from the road, if every gardenless town house had a tub of flowers at the door, every place would take on a happier, more colourful look. For flowers give a little smile to everyone who passes, making the day seem brighter all round. And gold really doesn't have to be only where we find it – it can be where we choose to put it.

A very happy New Year to you.

Flowers in December

From the garden: *Viburnum tinus* (laurustinus), last roses, decorative kale and cabbages, evergreen foliages, berries. **From the shops:** Anemones, gladioli, mimosa, carnations, *ranunculus*, white lilac, chrysanthemums.

Therefore all seasons shall be sweet to thee,
Whether the summer clothe the general earth
With greenness, or the redbreast sit and sing
Betwixt the tufts of snow on the bare branch
Of mossy apple tree . . .
Or if the secret ministry of frost
Shall hang them up in silent icicles,
Quietly shining to the quiet moon.

S. T. Coleridge   121

FLOWER ARRANGING
TERMS &
TECHNIQUES

A

Abstract

An abstract is a style of flower arranging, in which the arranger seeks to draw right away from the conventional, the familiar, breaking new ground and using plant materials in unconventional and unfamiliar ways. The emphasis is on strong, forceful design in which space is an important element. The end results are often handsome rather than pretty.

The abstract has been called 'the art of taking away', so that it becomes the exact opposite of the traditional massed arrangement. Dramatic linear patterns are encountered from which anything that could be considered superfluous has been taken away. Plant material is often altered, even distorted, and presented in exaggerated, unnaturalistic, exciting new ways, far removed from the way in which it grew.

Classes for expressive abstracts (where the plant material is set to work to interpret a theme) and decorative abstracts (in which the plant forms are used purely as elements in the design) are often found at shows and always create a talking point.

Accessory

An accessory in competitive flower arranging is anything other than the plant material, the container with its base or bases, and any drapes or backing. Accessories should be carefully chosen to 'go' with the style and character, colouring and size, of the overall design, and will often help portray a given show theme. Suitable accessories to place with flowers may be such things as a framed photograph, a book, a figurine, an artist's palette, an embroidery frame with wools to match the flowers, or a group of stones. Accessories may be placed inside the container or used elsewhere

in the space allowed, to give visual balance to the whole. They should be of secondary interest – plant material must always be the dominant factor, and the first thing to take the eye, in competitive work.

It is useful to remember that the printed word on a pure white background, perhaps used as a title card, can often be over-eye-catching in a show exhibit. The human face in a figurine can also draw the eye too much. A title written on soft-shaded card, and slightly turned in the niche, will carry the eye to the main part of the design. Figurines positioned so that they look away from the observer, preferably towards the flowers, have the same effect. Very shiny objects should be tried out first to see if they are too dominant. Fluffy toys and cheap-looking ornamental items never enhance any flowerpiece – even field flowers have quality, and though the accessory need not be costly it must always be of intrinsic good design.

B

Balance

A sense of visual balance is something with which we are all born. Few people can resist putting a crooked picture straight or doing something about a tilted curtain rail! This inbuilt desire for balance can be applied to a flower design.

When flower arrangers speak of balance they usually mean visual balance. To look pleasantly balanced, all the components of the arrangement must be assembled so that they appear to the eye to be of equal weight on either side of an imaginary central line. Some flowers and leaves appear visually heavier than others. Dark flowers usually look heavier than pale ones. Buds or sprays seem lighter than bold and eye-catching blooms and leaves. It is a fascinating business to visually balance one side with another, so that whether the plant materials on either side are very similar or entirely different, they will appear to be in complete visual accord – well balanced, as we say. Add a trifle overmuch, perhaps one too-heavy flower, and the observer gets the unpleasant feeling that the arrangement is about to tip over to that side. It can all be put right either by removing the offending item, replacing it with a visually lighter one, or by adding more 'weight' on the opposite side.

Balance is one of the most important elements in a good flower arrangement, whatever the chosen shape of

the design – whether symmetrical or asymmetrical, or whether the design is meant to be seen from the front or from all sides.

Bases

A base or bases placed underneath a flower container will often make all the difference to the finished effect, providing a look of stability and completeness to a design. It may be the means of linking flowers, container, and perhaps an accessory, together into one satisfying whole. It will often

a book, a tin, or whatever is handy, with a suitable drape.

Bases are often made from fabric-covered cake boards, available in various sizes – you can cover them yourself or sometimes buy them ready-covered at flower club sales tables; or they may be of draped fabric brought under the design. They can be slices of wood, antique stands, flat pieces of marble, slate or stone, trays, plates, or what you will. It is sometimes advantageous if the base is held slightly above table level, and this can

help the visual balance by adding just the right weight at the bottom. (At home, it will protect a table top.) A base can be of any shape, colour, or material, but should be chosen with care as to size so that it does not overwhelm the rest of the design or, on the contrary, appear so small and insignificant that it has no real role to play. In competitive work, bases are often important when used to give 'lift' to an exhibit. If, for instance, it is obvious that an arrangement needs to be higher in its niche, a spur-of-the-moment base can be made by covering

be done by gluing or screwing four corks underneath, or standing the base on four cotton reels.

NAFAS (National Association of Flower Arranging Societies) allows the use of bases in competitive work; bases are not classed as accessories.

Buds

Sometimes, because of the important role they play as pointed shapes for sketching-in the outline or silhouette of a design, we require buds to stay as they are for the life of the arrangement. A gathered rosebud will stay 125

tight and never open into a fully-blown flower if you gently ease the outer petals back and cover them generously with the lightly beaten white of an egg. Put the petals carefully back into place and then hold the bud firmly closed until the egg white sets. Tulips and iris can be held back similarly. The lifespan of the flower is not shortened so long as the actual handling of the flowerhead is gentle and managed with very cool (preferably moist) hands – I like to put my hands in cold water before touching the petals.

Iris can be held back for a day or so if each cut flower bud is gently bound

round with darning wool. There is no more miraculous sight than watching an iris bud expand, crisp and lovely, into a perfect bloom a few seconds after the band of wool is released.

When we want open roses and none are available we can open buds artificially. Choose buds which feel slightly soft to the touch and with the calyx (the outer green starry bit) beginning to curl back from the outer petals. Hold the flower loosely in the hand and blow hard into the top of the bud. Slowly the outer petals will begin to unfurl, and they can then be gently and individually curled back further. The petals will not tear if you continue blowing into the expanding flower, and if only the outside petals are turned back each time. If you are unable to find sufficient buds which are already feeling soft, stand well-coloured buds in hot water in a warm place. As the water cools, top up with more hot. It may take a day for the buds to mature sufficiently to be successfully opened as described above.

Fat tulip buds can be opened very easily by carefully smoothing the petals right back on themselves, one at a time between finger and thumb. You should not try this on very immature tulips for fear of cracking and soiling the petals. A tulip which has been opened artificially will look different from those which have opened naturally in the sun. Not everyone likes the effect, but the open flowers certainly make excellent focal points at a time of year when a few bold and eye-catching flowers may be valuable.

(To force budded branches open in late winter, see Forcing Blossoms.)

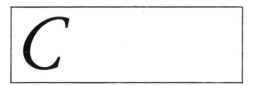

Candlecup

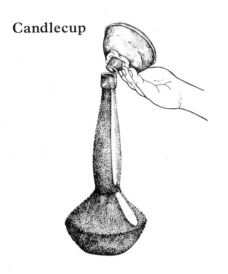

A candlecup is a shallow bowl-shaped container with a projecting stem which fits firmly into the neck of a candlestick or bottle. With the help of candlecups, simple everyday things can be turned into flower containers which lift the plant material and display it lightly and well. Candlecups can be filled with chicken wire or water-retaining foam. The water level should be checked daily, as the capacity of a candlecup is not very great. A simple alternative is to use a pilchard tin on top of a candlestick, securing the tin with modelling clay and a couple of stout rubber bands. Paint the tin to match the candlestick for best effect.

Chicken wire
Also called wire netting or wire mesh, chicken wire has been in use as an aid in massed flower arrangements at least since Gertrude Jekyll suggested it in the early part of the century. It can be bought by the yard or metre from ironmongers and garden shops. Buy the cheapest two-inch (50 mm) mesh – anything more rigid is too difficult to crumple up, while a smaller mesh will not allow all stems to be threaded through. Cut off, with pliers, a piece which will nicely fill your container when crumpled loosely together and will form a small dome above the rim of the container. Cut ends of wire can be hooked round any suitable rim or handle for extra security. One or two cut ends left upright at the centre back will be found invaluable for holding the main stems of the arrangement secure. Chicken wire can be held in place with strong rubber bands, or string, or florists' wire, or transparent sticky tape, which should be passed right round both the wire and the container, as though you were tying up a parcel. It should be secure enough to enable you to lift up the container by the wire.

Colour
Many books on art, interior design, and flower arrangement contain colour charts which may help to create pleasing colour schemes. *The NAFAS Guide to Colour Theory* is available through flower arrangement clubs. But though charts can be invaluable for the student or for the show exhibitor entering in special classes which relate to the use of colour, generally it is only by working thoughtfully and imaginatively with the flowers themselves, co-ordinating, **127**

blending and contrasting the living colours that we really begin to learn. In competitive flower arranging neutral colours are black, white and grey, by the way.

Competitive work

This is very special – usually interpretive designing for which the flower arranger is working to a given schedule and seeks perfection in all parts of the exhibit. When visitors to shows are heard to say 'I could never have that in my home' they are missing the point. Show exhibits are not arranged for the home, unless the schedule specifies something like 'an exhibit suitable for a country cottage supper table' or 'an exhibit for the summer hearth'. Show work is really an exercise in flower arranging, and the exhibitor pulls out all the stops and aims for imaginative excellence. Many designs are truly inspired works of art and should be seen and appreciated as such. Show work is a wonderful teacher and a great mind-stretcher, and the arranger is often able to bring off effects which could not have been imagined if she had simply arranged the same flowers at home.

Conditioning

The care of cut flowers and foliage begins the moment we walk into the garden to gather them. Choose the early morning, when plants are fully charged with moisture, or the evening, when they have the highest food reserves. If neither time is practical, try to gather after light rain or some time after plants have been well

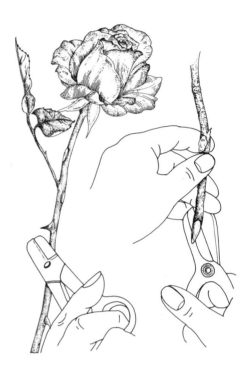

watered. The very worst time to pick flowers and leaves is on hot dry days with the sun directly on them. Make a long slanting cut, using sharp flower-gathering scissors or a knife, and put immediately into a jug or bucket of tepid water which you have taken into the garden with you. Put wild flowers into a plastic bag which has been lightly dampened inside.

If flowers are cut straight into water it will not usually be necessary to provide a pre-arrangement drink of shallow hot water, unless the plant material is soft and tender or is a known difficult subject like very young foliage, lilac, gerbera, hellebore, or wild flowers. Drinks of very hot water are given to rid stems of airlocks which prevent the passage of water and so make the flowers or leaves flag. Once indoors, leave

glycerine dissolved in three table-spoonsful of hot water.

Cut flowers

Over the years arrangers have devised many ways of helping their cut flowers to last well, though I would say there is nothing better than cutting straight into clear water! But try the methods out for yourself. *Try*:

★ Adding a teaspoonful of sugar or glucose, dissolved in warm water, to the water in the container for roses.

★ A two to four seconds' dip-drink in peppermint oil for roses, honeysuckle, Solomon's seal, gerbera, dahlia, hosta, and tamarisk.

★ Two-minute drinks of vinegar for wild flowers before arranging them.

★ A three-second drink of neat gin (for the flowers rather than yourself!), or use a specially formulated cut flower food such as Chrysal in the container, for any cut flowers and leaves.

When using alcohol, vinegar, or peppermint oil, first wipe the flower stems dry, leave for a few minutes without water, then dip in the solution. Leave no longer than the stated times or the life-span will be shortened rather than prolonged.

Try:

★ Dipping the cut ends of summer flower stems, particularly dahlias, into cooking salt before arranging (this is to disinfect the stems and help the intake of water).

★ Singeing the base of the stems of euphorbias, poinsettias, poppies, and other plants which drip latex when cut (hold them in a gas flame

flowers and foliage to have a long deep drink for some hours in a cool place before arranging them. This is not, of course, always very practicable for homely flower decorations, but recutting the stem ends under water as you remove them from the gathering jug or bucket is important, and it is an obvious advantage to arrange such material in deep containers which have a good water-holding capacity.

Foliage

Foliage can be difficult, particularly when immature. Give it a good deep drink of warm water in which you have dissolved a little glycerine (about a tablespoonful to every half pint of water). In autumn, cut branches hold on to their foliage a little longer if they are sprayed (using a small flower and plant sprayer) with a tablespoonful of

for a few moments until the stem seals), because this again is said to disinfect the stem and allow warm air to escape and thus increase the water-drawing capacity.

Woody stems

Woody stems such as lilac, roses, and sprays of leaves need special care and relish a drink in boiling shallow water after the stem ends have been split open and scraped.

Hellebores and other difficult subjects can usually be persuaded to take up water – at least at some stage in their lives, when hellebores are showing seedheads, for example – after a shallow hot-water drink.

Soft stems are damaged by very hot water so it must be shallow.

Flowerheads should be protected from steam.

Revival tips

If garden flowers are found to have flagged badly on a hot day they can generally be revived if you hold them upside down in the sink and plenty of cool water is poured gently over them. Then wrap them completely in a sheet of newspaper and pour water over it so that it too becomes moist. Leave the flowers lying flat in a cool, light place and within an hour they will have recharged with moisture and look fresh once more.

Some people like to float wilted plant material in water for about an hour.

Carnations should be cut above the hard bit where the leaves join the stem.

Containers – general

Antique or modern, costly or junk, home-made or bought, recognisable at once as something of use for holding flowers or not, containers come in every shape and size and range from such things as thimbles for tiny miniature arrangements, to enormous urns for cathedral-size designs. Whatever it is, if it is used to arrange and display flowers or other plant forms, it is known among arrangers as a container. If it will not hold water it can still be useful for fruits, preserved flowers and so on, or it may be provided with a dish or bowl to hold water. Sometimes we can use household items such as cooking and serving dishes, hair spray lids, mugs, decanters, spoons, Mother's old cake stand or Granny's old Bible box. As antiques grow more expensive and hard to find, and with good modern

pots also commanding high prices, arrangers have adapted to all kinds of novel and cheap containers.

In many arrangements today the container is hidden and plays no visual part. Shallow workaday containers, completely covered by the plant material, are very popular, plastic plant pot saucers being ideal as they come in all sorts of sizes right up to 18-inch (45 cm) for terrace pots. The green ones and the brown are easiest to disguise. Most are deep enough to hold a pinholder, chicken wire, or a wedge of one of the flower foams for fresh or preserved flowers. In competitive work it is vital to make the container always subordinate to the flowers, which is why a hidden container can be a triumph and why some containers are too beautiful for their own good! At a show beware of things which shine or glow overmuch, are very ornate and patterned, or too highly coloured. The effect of an over-dominant container can at times be minimised by bringing a few flowers, leaves, fruits, or a branch across the front, or by slightly turning the container in its space.

Stemmed containers like candle-sticks, figurines holding bowls, and so on, always display flowers well, giving them a lively lift and allowing a soft downward flow. They are useful for buffet tables, show niches, or whenever an arrangement has to be raised to be seen.

Containers should always be kept scrupulously clean and never be put away dirty after use. Clean the insides with wire wool and brushes.

Creating curves

Flower arrangers often prefer bending, slightly twisting shapes to perfect upright lines. Lupins, stocks, and snapdragons will curve lightly if left overnight leaning at an angle over the rim of their deep-drink bucket of water. Float gladioli overnight in deep water, and in the morning the tips will have taken on a softly curving line. Evergreens, pussy willow, and flowering or leafy branches can be coaxed into curves by applying gentle pressure with long smooth movements along the stem, but not at a joint. Broom tied into a circle will set into a softer line when released. 131

D

Design

In flower arranging the words design or overall design specifically refer to the manner in which various items of plant material are assembled together to make harmony with container, any accessories, and background. The outline or silhouette of the design is always important and is generally 'sketched in' first or very early. Proportion and scale are clearly important in designing anything and, particularly in a show flower arrangement, the height and width of the silhouette should be carefully considered. Always keep outlines airy and light. The components of design basically fall into three main categories: pointed shapes, round shapes, and in-between shapes. When these shapes with their colours and textures are interplayed well together in the space allowed, a good design will be composed. (See also Balance, Focal Points, Containers.)

Drapes and backgrounds

Drapes, as pieces of suitable fabric used in conjunction with flower designs, are rather out of favour at the moment except as accompaniments to pedestals, where they are quite often seen at shows. However, backgrounds of paper-covered or fabric-covered wood, strong card, etc, sometimes lightly painted, are much in fashion for competitive work. Unless prohibited by the schedule, they are allowed as part of an exhibit and not classed as accessories. Whatever is used in this way should slip into the overall design quietly, not taking up too prominent and eye-catching a role. A background of hardboard, supported by two screwed-on brackets which act as feet at the back, can help to portray a theme or title by being painted with poster paints to suggest a distant misty view, the sea, sky, or what you will. These free-standing backgrounds usually look best with gently-rounded top corners, which are softer on the eye than hard squared edges, but cut-outs of various shapes are also possible, and for modern work voids or empty spaces cut into a background can be effective. Before starting to make a background from any material it is sensible to make quite sure of the height of any niche or backdrop which is to be provided at the show (the show schedule should give you information on this) and it is well to stay an inch or so lower.

High windows – in churches, for example – make difficult backgrounds, for the light source is wrong. In such conditions, with most of the light behind the arrangement (unless spotlights can be fitted up), bold flowers, and well-defined outlines, will often be the most effective solution.

In the home, a plain or quietly patterned background to a flower arrangement will usually be an advantage. But in a room which has bold patterned wallpaper or many pictures, it helps to place the arrangement some distance from the wall so that the background becomes less obtrusive and sets off the flowers. Similarly the

trick of setting them against a dark area of painting can be advantageous. Standing the arrangement in front of a mirror is often pleasing, but of course the back of the design must also be good to look at because it will be reflected in the glass.

Placing the arrangement against a non-patterned curtain is another answer to the patterned wall question, and it pays to choose large and dramatically coloured flowers or dominating plain leaves in these circumstances.

Driftwood

Driftwood is the blanket term used for any dried wood and it includes the bark of trees and their roots too. Driftwood does not necessarily have to come from the sea – it can be found all over the place – in woods, hedgerows, and gardens. Pieces of twisted ivy or wistaria are specially ap-preciated by flower arrangers though they may have to be scraped to expose the smooth inner wood.

Dirt or rotted wood should be scraped or brushed away when you get your treasure home. The piece must then be scrubbed with a strong solution of detergent and then, when dry, it is vital to treat it with a woodworm killer. The wood may be left natural, or polished with a cloth, bleached by leaving it in a solution of bleach for a few days, or coloured in various ways (with dark stain shoe polish, shoe dye, poster paint). If the piece will not stand firmly it can usually be persuaded to do so – for instance, it may be possible to screw it to a suitable base or to wedge or stick it to another piece of driftwood. There are special metal gadgets available, but a wide-pinned pinholder may support driftwood steadily.

E

Exhibit

This is a word you will meet as soon as you begin to interest yourself in competitive flower arranging. It means an arrangement, or more than one arrangement, of plant material, with which an accessory, or more than one accessory, may be used – or not, as you please. An exhibit 'of natural plant material only' means exactly what it says; no accessories to be used. 'An exhibit to include one accessory' means your showpiece will be disqualified as 'Not according to schedule' if you pop in two accessories or none at all. So it really is worth while to read the show schedule with care, for all schedules are different.

F

Figurines

Figurines made of metal, china, wood, etc, in the form of birds, animals, fish, or humans can be very effectively linked with flowers. In competitive classes, where they are often used to help interpret a given theme, figurines must always play second fiddle to the plant material. As with any accessory, a figurine which is too large or otherwise dominant may put out the whole balance of a design, for example by creating an eye-catching focal point in the wrong place.

Florists' flowers

When we spend money on buying flowers we naturally wish them to last as long as possible. Funny things can happen to flowers nowadays, particularly round about traditional festivals such as Christmas, Easter, and Mother's Day, when some flowers are deliberately held back in cold store so as to hit the shops at the most profitable time. Thus treated, very delicate spring flowers may curl up their petals and die off very quickly. Never buy anything which is in any way suspect, languid-looking, with even slight browning on petals or leaves, or which puts the slightest doubt in your mind at first sight. A good florist will treat the flowers correctly so that they are in perfect condition when you get them home. 'Perfect condition' means sturdy water-charged stems and leaves, clear colours, and with flowers

such as freesias, spray carnations and spray chrysanthemums there should be plenty of fat buds still waiting to come out.

Roses, tulips, paeonies, iris, are best bought in bud, as are daffodils. When buying dahlias or chrysanthemums look at the backs of the blooms; the petals should be crisp and not falling. Centres of double varieties should be tight and in-curving. These are just a few examples but they serve as a good general guide. Any flowers normally sold with their leaves, such as chrysanthemums, must be suspect if the leaves have been stripped away – they have probably been in the shop for many days. Re-cut the stem ends of all florists' flowers and leaves when you get them home and you can arrange them immediately.

Florists' tubes

Florists' tubes are slim, cone-shaped metal tubes of various sizes, often sold at flower club sales tables. They can be invaluable when arranging massed flowers in large containers, when extra height is required and the stems of the available flowers or branches are not quite long enough. They are also particularly useful for pedestal arrangements. Lightly filled with chicken wire, with damp Oasis or, in emergency, a few short pieces of cut twig material or flower stem, the larger tubes hold sufficient water to support a number of quite thick stalks.

Each tube must first be prepared for use by attaching it with transparent sticky tape or wire to a long piece of stick, and if helpful to the design more than one tube can be attached to one

stick. For large arrangements, such as pedestals, it is a good plan to buy slim yet sturdy square-cut wood from a do-it-yourself shop rather than to use something round, such as a tomato

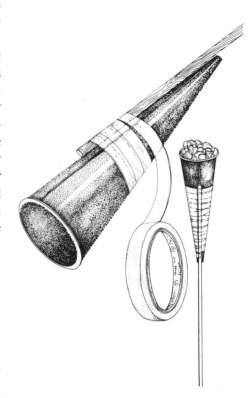

cane, which may have a tendency to be whippy and to bend slightly out of line, particularly when supporting heavy branches or tall flowers such as gladioli. A piece of the support stick left above the tube itself can be useful – a wayward branch, for instance, can be tied to it. After attaching the tube to its stick, wire a few sprays of conifer discreetly around the stick so that in use it will be invisible. When placing the tube in the arrangement, press the end of the stick down 135

through chicken wire and on to a pinholder very firmly, then wire the stick in place. It is vital that it be secure; a few cut ends of the chicken wire can be twisted round the stick for extra safety. For a big pedestal arrangement, greater security can be provided – and each tube held really firm – with four 'arms' of strong reel wire taken round each stick several turns then down to each corner of the container.

There are other tubes which will add height for the odd flower stem; they can be made from metal cigar cases and travelling toothbrush cases. Orchid tubes (many good florists have these and throw them away!) are handy used just as they are when a little extra plant material is required with fruit or in a pot-et-fleur. The fact that an orchid tube has a rubber seal top with a hole in it, through which the stem is pressed, makes it ideal even for positions which call for a stem to be upside down.

Flower arrangement clubs

Addresses of flower clubs in your area can usually be obtained from the public library, or you can inquire from the London headquarters of the National Association of Flower Arrangement Societies, the parent body; send a stamped, addressed envelope. (See NAFAS.)

Flower arranging

Although specifically mentioning flowers, the blanket term 'flower arranging' in truth covers all plant forms which are used decoratively by arrangers. Unless a show schedule asks for any specific plant material we may use foliage, fruit, bracts, seaweed, grasses, pulses, etc, for our effects.

Flower festivals

During the past decade many thousands of pounds have been raised for charities large and small by flower arrangers who have organised successful flower festivals in churches and cathedrals, stately homes, manor houses, civic centres, and so on. No matter whether a festival is to be big or a very small affair, it is necessary to get a committee together if possible twelve months ahead of the chosen date as there is much to plan – and flower arrangers' diaries do tend to get very full. A local flower arrangement club may well be happy to undertake a festival for a church or at least will send a representative to advise, for most clubs have acquired a lot of know-how. If possible, plan the festival for a flowery time of year, when garden plant material will be readily available. The committee, with its appointed chairman, should visit the festival venue and, with tape measures and notebooks, carefully plan each exhibit.

Working to an overall theme is interesting for exhibitors and public alike. The theme may be suggested by the history of the building, by its nature and the work it does, by its colour schemes, or by its furnishings and decorations. From the start, the people in charge of the chosen building must be consulted and be kept abreast of plans. They will sometimes assist by providing money towards flowers and they should always be

responsible for such things as car parking, publicity, refreshments, toilets and, at stately homes, etc, crowd control (which may have to include liaison with the police and the AA if the festival is to be a big affair). Small church festivals can be even more interesting if, say, a whole village can go *en fête* with gardens thrown open to the public and flowers arranged in all the shop windows.

Helpful instructions in writing should be given to each arranger in good time, and a meeting set up for the arrangers to visit the building with the committee to see where they will be arranging their flowers, where the water will be, and so on. It is most important to create a happy atmosphere, and special consideration should be given to each arranger on staging and clearing days; they should have free passes to all the events, and free car parking. Finally, exhibitors appreciate a letter of thanks afterwards, giving details of the money raised and the success of the festival on which they have lavished so much time and thought.

Flower foams

One of the 'mechanics' of flower arranging is special water-absorbing foam, sold under various trade names including Oasis. After being cut to fit the container – and an inch or so higher than the container's rim – it is soaked in warm water for not longer than ten minutes. In that time a complete block of Oasis will absorb about three pints of water. It can be used for some time until the foam breaks up or becomes too full of holes. It should

not be allowed to dry out while in use, or it will suck moisture out from the plant material! Once soaked, keep it damp in a plastic bag after use as it sometimes breaks up or is difficult to charge with water again if it dries out. Oasis can be covered first with thin clear plastic or kitchen foil and then with chicken wire, leaving a hook by which it can be hung, and used as an invisible holder for flowers when decorating pew ends for a wedding, for example, or a font or lectern.

Styrofoam is a green, white, or brown foam of slightly firmer substance than Oasis, used dry to hold stems of preserved subjects and silk flowers. It does not absorb water, but otherwise is used in exactly the same way as Oasis. It can be bought in a variety of shapes, from which Christmas decorations can be made, which are really rather different.

Focal points

The focal point of an arrangement is the centre of visual weight at its heart. All the stems should appear to radiate from here. In traditional work it usually lies at the centre front of the design just above the rim of the container. It is the strongest, most characterful area of the design. Round shapes, such as open roses, or flowers

growing in eye-catching clusters, such as rhododendrons, make very suitable focal points. A common fault in traditional work is to make the focal point play too forceful a role in the design, so that the eye is immediately drawn to it and cannot easily escape. This may occur when using a figurine or other accessory as the focal point. Invariably a few plain, well-shaped leaves set around this area improves a design, creating an area of calm and rest.

Things to avoid: one bloom of a different sort from all the rest; one flower or fruit much larger than anything else in the design; one item of very shiny texture when everything else is matt.

In abstract and very modern work, breaking with traditional styles, the arrangement may have more than one focal point or area of interest. These can be very visually dominant indeed. The focal point might even be simply one or more spaces enclosed by plant material, taking its inspiration from modern sculpture.

Foliage

Even those without a garden should somehow scheme to grow a few plants with good leaves which they can cut from time to time, or take walks into the country to make small gatherings of leaves, for almost every flower arrangement is better for accompanying foliage. Indeed, whole designs can be made from leaves, and houseplants, tub plants, and garden plants are wonderful providers of foliage when well grown. Nobody can grow everything (though some of us try) but if our space is really very limited we do well to base our selection on those plants with the bold, the plain-coloured, the very well tailored, crisply shaped leaves, in preference to the over-fussy and highly patterned, for these latter kinds will have more limited use. Leaves which are strong and bold, with few frills or flounces, broken surface patterning, or any kind of

fidgety effect, make invaluable cut plant material. They act as a foil to fussy flowers with many overlapping petals, like zinnias and carnations, or very cut-up frilly leaves, like most of the ferns. Aspidistras, hostas, New Zealand flax (phormium), iris, begonia, and plain-coloured ivy leaves spring at once to mind as 'good' leaves for our purpose.

Useful leaves include *Fatsia japonica*, ivy, vines, bergenia, hosta, skimmia, anemone, geranium, and *Alchemilla mollis*. Good pointed shapes include New Zealand flax, yucca, pittosporum, perennial poppies, iris, sprays of ivy, beech, ferns, heathers, Solomon's seal, griselinia, privet, snowdrop.

Forcing blossoms

Branches of spring blossom such as forsythia, cherry, amelanchier, flowering currant, mahonia, etc, can be brought into early flower if you cut well-budded branches in late winter or early spring. Flower buds are usually just visible, as round rather than pointed buds, along the branches. Cut the branches thoughtfully, selecting well-shaped pieces to fit the design you have in mind. Cut a few stems over a period of some weeks and you can get continuity of opening buds, though obviously the closer to the normal opening time the sooner will the flower buds be forced open. Stand the branches in a warm place in a container of hot water, keeping it filled with more hot water each day. If the branches are very beautifully shaped and attractive in their own right they can often be used straightaway in an arrangement, perhaps with other flowers, as you wait for the buds to expand. If forced in the dark, flowering currant will produce ethereal white flowers instead of pink.

Frontal arrangements

A frontal arrangement is one which is designed to be viewed mainly face-on by a person of average height. Popular at flower arrangement shows, where it is often displayed in a niche of a given size, the frontal arrangement is also most useful at home for a position in a corner, against a wall, or in an alcove. 139

Although it is designed to be viewed mainly from the front, few positions call for a design which has only one attractive face. All designs (other than those made of pressed flowers) by their very nature have some depth to them and will be seen often from the side as we walk towards them, so this view too should be planned.

When arranging a frontal design, allow some flowers, leaves, or branches to flow down, and out at the sides, bring some forward over the rim towards you, and recess others in towards the chicken wire, foam, or pinholder. Similarly, place some stems to the back of the design to help the visual balance when seen from the side. All this gives a three-dimensional effect, an in-and-out movement, and a feeling of liveliness. Though of secondary importance to the front view, the sides of the design should always be attractive, balanced, and well-finished. Often when judging show classes where there are two or three exhibits of almost equal merit competing for a prize, the judge will be able to decide between them when she compares their side-view artistry.

Usually, to turn a design slightly in its space is advantageous, as the container and base are seen from a more interesting angle; this gets over any flat-fronted, sliced-off effect which is dullness itself! By turning some flowers to show side or back views and using others face-on, and by choosing plant materials which have depth within themselves (eg bell-shaped flowers), or by arranging together dark and light material, you can make a good three-dimensional effect.

140

H

Hogarth Curve

The Hogarth Curve, or 'the line of beauty', is the name given to the softly curving line inspired by the eighteenth-century painter and engraver William Hogarth, who abhorred forms based on static geometrical or mathematical principles. In 1745 he painted a portrait of himself and his dog Trump. In the picture is a palette on which Hogarth has drawn a serpentine line, with the words 'the line of beauty'. The line appears in the pic-

Self-portrait with his dog Trump by William Hogarth. The painting, which features the palette with the 'line of beauty' or Hogarth Curve, hangs in the Tate Gallery, London.

ture as a lazy, undulating movement, rather like an S; it is equally beautiful when copied in flower arrangements as an ordinary letter S or as a reversed S-shape.

The Hogarth Curve is usually seen in an arrangement in a stemmed container of some kind, as this allows the lower part of the line to stay clear of the table, but it also makes a most satisfactory shape when arranged horizontally for a table decoration. Long pointed material is required for the outline of the shape, and stems may be coaxed into suitable curves by smoothing them gently in both hands between fingers and thumbs. A piece of flower foam makes a good support for the stems. When creating an upright S-shaped arrangement the top curve is positioned first (one-and-a-half to twice the height of the container). Place it towards the centre back, with its tip over the spot which will be the centre of interest, or focal point. Next define the lower curve of the S, and bring its tip gently down and round so that it visually balances the top curve. Place a few large flowers towards the centre of the design, backed by well-shaped leaves, and fill in with more plant material, making quite sure that you keep everything within the somewhat tailored confines of the S-shaped outline.

Flower arrangement purists sometimes argue as to whether the Hogarth Curve should really ever be a reversed S. It seems however that Hogarth painted the portrait in reverse because he intended it to be turned into a printing plate for an engraving (the scar on his brow is in reverse). It is therefore arguable which way round he saw his 'line of beauty' – but as both the ordinary S-shape and the reversed form appear strongly in his work. I believe he thought both to be as good.

Home arrangements

If the average woman's day is to include time for flower arranging, time for relaxing for a refreshing moment or two with flowers, then we must look for methods of arrangement which are as quick and simple to do as possible, while still giving pleasure to the eye and the spirit. In this way we can enjoy having flowers around us all the time, not just on occasion. Used very simply and unaffectedly, every kind of flower is absolutely in tune

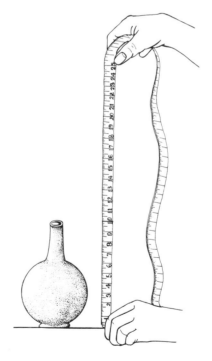

When using a tall container, the first placement, the tallest stem, should be $1\frac{1}{2}$ to 2 times the height of the container. 141

with life today; used in ways which make them seem over-arranged, too much on their best behaviour, they appear out of step, dated, show-benchy.

Now is the time to rethink our everyday flowers by gearing down and simplifying long-established ideas – which may be a rather difficult step for the experienced arranger to take, but not every design has to be a work of art! Display a single branch or a few blooms just as specimens, and look at and admire them for themselves alone. Uncontrived neatly bunched posies, small gatherings of garden or country things massed simply into a pleasing container without the aid of chicken wire or Oasis, can give great pleasure, will last a long time and are quickly replaced. Floating flowerheads in a low container is another 'quickie' method and very 'art deco'!

Ikebana

The student of Ikebana (the Japanese art of flower arrangement) learns to create harmonious, well-balanced arrangements according to certain clearly laid down methods and rules. These are passed directly from master to teacher to student. There is even conformity in the way notes must be written down at lessons, and only as the student advances is she allowed to try out her own ideas within the school's discipline. The work is un-

usual, often very dramatic, but always with a general air of the restrained and beautiful. There is classical Ikebana and modern Ikebana, and students are taught every aspect of their art. This includes the skills of bending and pruning cut branches to achieve a perfect line. It is always interesting to see other traditions and styles, and I believe Ikebana has much to offer and teach the Western flower arranger.

Interpretive exhibit

A design which interprets a given theme, tells a story, or portrays a mood.

Landscapes

Landscape designs, although generally encountered in shows, can be equally interesting to do at home. They are scaled-down landscapes and seascapes, table-size natural scenes of moorland, wood, desert, and river bank. To make a true landscape involves being able to shrink in imagi-

nation so that a branch suggests a bending tree, a few stones some amazing rock formation, a trifle of light-reflecting water a woodland or garden pool with mosses seeming like grass. A curl of driftwood becomes a sheltering cave for a small animal, or perhaps a snow-covered slope for a tiny ski-ing figure at Christmastime. Seascapes are suitable pebbles, succulents, etc, to suggest a seashore or underwater scene. Indeed, the plant material though not necessarily of the area you are portraying should undoubtedly clearly suggest it. For example, sophisticated florists' flowers are not a good choice for a moorland landscape nor wild flowers for a garden setting.

Accessories as well as plant material should be to scale and in character, with water creatures used in a watery setting – and not a lady in a crinoline gown! Home-made signposts, stiles, garden gates, and so on, can be easily made, and help set the scene. Bases made of chipboard, ridged cardboard, linen, etc, may suggest earth or sand, and suitable low dishes of an earthy colour, left clear for water, can be useful as miniature lakes and quiet rivers.

Line arrangements

These are the opposite of massed arrangements. In the latter, many flowers are massed together for effect. A line design is more restrained, uses fewer flowers, and relies for effect on a well-defined, clear-cut linear shape. The line must, of course, be an interesting one and will use space as a planned part of the design. Line arrangements are suited to any sophisti-cated form of furnishing, antique or modern, and will also look effective with an oriental-style decor. The country cottage style of furnishing and decoration is less suitable as a setting.

As the flowers and leaves are few in number, each must be placed with great care. Each must play its part in the development of the design. In the best line arrangements every detail of the material has a part in the design – the tilt of a petal, the line of a leaf, the twist of a stem is used so effectively as part of the design that the visual impression of them is heightened. Looking at such an arrangement, one might be seeing all flowers, leaves and stems clearly and revealingly for the very first time. When this feeling occurs you have undoubtedly created a work of art.

M

Massed arrangements

The traditional English massed flower arrangement is much admired throughout the world. It presents the eye with a richness of shape instead of the strongly controlled linear emphasis of the line arrangement. Material is used in greater abundance and many fine and varied effects can be achieved. (See 'May', page 54.) The style fits happily with the decor of all homes except perhaps the strikingly ultra-modern.

When decorating churches, large halls, or rooms for public functions, the mass arrangement really comes into its own, for it is colourful, eye-catching, and understood by all. Mass arrangements can be quite sophisticated or perfectly homely and simple. As with line designs, you can take advantage of the subtle personalities of flowers and leaves, their textures, shapes, and colours, to build up beautiful and satisfying designs.

I believe all flower arrangers can become proficient at both line and mass arrangements, though not all succeed equally well with both – perhaps because people usually develop a fondness for one or the other and do their best work with it.

Mechanics

The so-called mechanics of flower arrangement are the various things which are used to hold and control stems, etc. They include wooden sticks screwed or glued to driftwood to help it stand securely, and special metal clamps sold for the same purpose, as well as the basic pinholders, flower foams, chicken wire, florists' tubes, and so on. (See also separate headings for these items.)

Miniatures

A miniature for competition must measure no more than four inches in height, depth, or width – and the judge will actually check the measurements! Some show committees have a card cut out to the correct dimensions, against which competitors can measure their exhibits.

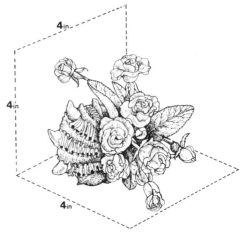

In an exhibit so reduced in size, a grass blade will appear as important as an iris leaf, a single escallonia flower like a fully-open rose. Every smallest item must be scaled down, including the container. Often at shows people use containers which are far too large. Eggcups, for example, seem enormous. Choose instead such things as tiny sea shells, bottle tops, flat buttons (as bases), miniature toy wheelbarrows and carts, and so forth. Bases

must not be so large as to overwhelm the tiny flower-piece, and if a class for a miniature is to include accessories, suitable items can often be found in toy and model shops; you can even use cake decorations and so on. Design a miniature exactly as you would a full-size arrangement, with plant material chosen in precisely the same way, to play the same role in the design. Many rockery plants provide ideal material, as do dwarf conifers, but anything with small enough flowers or foliage can be used.

As tiny containers may not hold very much water, it is obviously an advantage if you can use plant material which has a built-in sturdiness or water-holding ability. Very delicate or flimsy little flowers or infant leaves may prove tricky and it is worth while to test things beforehand and see how they will perform under stress conditions.

For rhythm within the design such things as clematis and vine tendrils, small stems of contorted hazel, and similar things, will add life and movement. From the greenhouse, miniature succulents and *Hoya carnosa* flowers might be gathered. Preserved bits and pieces have a clear advantage over fresh material, though some competitions do insist on the material being fresh. Stems can be held in place in flower foam which has been wired or stuck into position. Some containers will take a few twists of florists' reel wire, used in the same way as chicken wire in a normal-size decoration. Some people like to use tweezers, cocktail sticks, or the points of nail scissors to assemble these

minute flowerpieces, and an eye-dropper can be a useful stand-in for the usual watering-can.

When positioning a miniature in a show you will usually have an eye-level stand on which to display it. Show cards which are smaller than usual should be used by show committees to give a more attractive overall effect to miniature classes. The cards should not, as is often the way, be placed under the exhibits, for fear of disturbing them when prize-winners' stickers or stars are put in position.

Modern arrangements

Modern arrangements are in tune with current ideas in architecture and furnishing. The same principles of visual balance, colour harmony, etc, still apply, but focal points are often directed away from the familiar traditional areas, and space is actively used within the design to 'balance' solids. 145

N

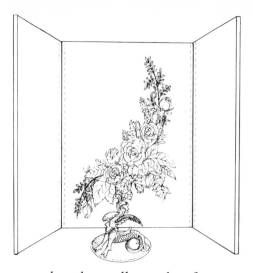

NAFAS

Most flower arrangement clubs are affiliated to the National Association of Flower Arrangement Societies (NAFAS), which trains and tests judges, demonstrators, and lecturers to the very highest standards. NAFAS aims to foster the love of flowers and to demonstrate their decorative value in the home. This remarkable organisation, which was founded in 1959, has over 100,000 individual members, and there are clubs in most towns and cities – some places have more than one. Subscriptions vary according to the circumstance of the club. Lists of accredited area and national judges and demonstrators, and copies of the NAFAS *Handbook of Schedule Definitions* may be bought from NAFAS, 21a Denbigh Street, London SW1, price 10p, at time of going to press. A letter to the Secretary at the same address, enclosing a stamped, addressed envelope, will bring details of any clubs in your neighbourhood. Newly published by NAFAS is the *Judges' Manual*, for the guidance of judges, exhibitors, show organisers and stewards, price £1 plus postage.

Niches

You will probably first come across references to niches or alcoves in a flower arrangement club show schedule. Where niches are provided they will be already *in situ* when you arrive to do your exhibit. Open-topped and usually made of corrugated card, board, or wood, they will be of the size and colour stated in the schedule. Therefore you can plan your exhibit beforehand so that it will 'sit' the niche attractively. Think of the niche as being the backing and the frame to the design you are creating. As with a picture in its frame, leave a little open space between the exhibit and the walls of the niche. If you think of the space within the niche as your empty canvas you will see that the whole of the space must come into your designing. I find it helpful when judging – or exhibiting – to imagine the niche roughly divided in two down the centre; as with all flower arrangements, there should be good visual balance at both sides. Most niches are taller than they are wide, so that tall arrangements or ones which are raised in some way become necessary for a well-planned effect. Bases, drapes, and home-made backgrounds can be of great help in achieving this unless a schedule specifically bars the use of a drape or background.

P

Pedestals

A pedestal is generally an elegantly-shaped column or plinth made of metal, marble or wood. It carries or holds at its top a container. A simple pedestal could be made from, say, a slim piece of tree trunk firmly fixed to a base. Sometimes a wine or coffee table can function as a small pedestal to hold a scaled-down pedestal arrangement – something of a most useful size for the average home – and can provide good practice for bigger pedestals.

Pedestal flower arrangements are usually in traditional symmetrical or asymmetrical designs. Arranged singly, or as a pair perhaps at either side of the chancel steps for a wedding, they have great presence and beauty. Pedestal arrangements may be of fresh or dried plant material or a mixture of both.

The mechanics for a pedestal – chicken wire, water-retaining foam, pinholder or florists' tubes – must be absolutely firm in the container before work on the arrangement is begun. For a large pedestal, which is to have flowers raised high in florists' tubes – it is a good idea first to place a strong pinholder at the back of the container; this will hold the stick of the tubes firmly. A block of Oasis, or more than one if necessary, goes in at the centre, wedged in by two smaller blocks at the sides. Then chicken wire is taken right over the top, scrunched down over the

pinholder at the back and into any space left at the front, but with a low dome left above the container's rim. When this is firmly wired to the container or pedestal it will hold anything you choose to put into it.

A three-footed pedestal should be positioned with two of the feet at the back and one at the front for strength, balance, and a nicely poised effect.

There are many ways of tackling the arrangement itself. It is usual to begin with the tallest 'backbone' stem (which can be raised in a florists' tube), then to bring in a flowing side stem at either side, plus three, four, or even five or more sprays, cut somewhat shorter, which skirt down at the front and out at the back, taking a low and gentle line. The design is then filled in, in the usual way (see Massed 147

Arrangements and Triangles). Bold shapes in flowers and leaves, rather than small or fussy ones, are very necessary in pedestal arrangements, which are usually meant to be seen from a distance; indeed, when pedestal classes are judged at shows, judges are recommended to stand four feet away.

Period exhibits

All period work must capture the general spirit, the 'flavour' of some past era. Flowers, foliage and containers of the present day are allowed so long as they suggest the atmosphere of the chosen period. Here are some periods which figure in competitive work and could inspire ideas for home flower arrangements.

Ancient Egyptian

Our guides for these arrangements are the frescoes, garlands and other ornamentation found in the tombs of ancient Egypt. The arrangements are stylised with fruits and flowers used in a very ordered and symmetrical fashion. Containers, such as bowls made of pottery, bronze, silver or gold, hold such flowers as the sacred blue lotus (water-lily) with its leaves and buds. Very tall, slim containers with spouts all the way up display leaves, flowers and fruits in evenly-spaced patterns which show off the strong bold shapes. Bunched bouquets (set in holders somewhat like ice-cream cones!) sometimes feature fruits held on slim sticks pressed through the centres of the flowers to make new shapes. Favourite colours are soft reds, blues, greens, orange, black and yellow.

Greek and Roman

Wreaths, chaplets and garlands of leaves and fruits were favoured for decorating pillars and doors and for carrying or wearing in processions. Heaped baskets of scented flowers for strewing, and upright cornucopias with flowers, fruits, and leaves clustered in the top will suggest the period. In the Vatican, a Roman mosaic of prettily-arranged flowers has roses, anemones, pinks and other flowers; it dates from the first century AD.

Byzantine

Stylised cone shapes, held in classic vases, with bright fruits, succulents, flowerheads and leaves make charming designs at Christmas and other seasons, using a cone of dry or water-absorbent foam as a base for the stems. Elegant containers of enamel, onyx and gilded metal studded with 'gems' are useful for the right effect, which should be one of perfect symmetry.

Flemish groups

Often exhibited at shows, these handsome flower decorations are based on the flowerpieces of the old Dutch and Flemish master painters. Originally painted throughout a whole season,

the pictures show such mixtures as summer roses with autumn corn and spring tulips. There are times in early summer when it is just possible to catch such flowers in bloom together, and with preserved corn, etc, the effect can be very good, otherwise the attempt should be to capture the impression of the fullness and richness of the paintings, not forgetting the empty snail shells, birds' nests with their eggs, butterflies, a watch on a ribbon to suggest the quick passage of time. Accessories are often balanced by the use of large flowers at the top of the arrangement. Containers and bases similar at least in feeling to those in the pictures should be chosen.

Georgian and Regency

Flower-filled baskets garlanded with ribbons and ropes of flowers, bunched posies in cornucopias; these are indicative of the elegance and delicate beauty of the period, as shown in fabrics and painted ceilings. From contemporary paintings, we know that urn-shaped containers held fresh and dried bunches, and 'bough pots', filled with flowers and leaves, decked the fireplaces in summer. Many fine vases of the period still linger on in stately homes and museums and a close study of their shapes gives an indication of the way flowers were actually arranged, for there is always the possibility that painters may have romanticised reality. However, for competitive work, some enchanting 'romantic' flowerpieces can be achieved.

For Regency designs, any reference to the popular Chinoiserie of the day gives authenticity.

Victorian

Flowers arranged in epergnes, tall 'trumpet' vases, glass of every sort, urns and other classic shapes, 'finger' vases, baskets fashioned in every kind of material, and so on, all suggest this period. The greatest care was taken by the Victorians to procure the richest and most extravagant effects for dinner parties and other social occasions, and exotic plant material was often selected to match the colours of not only the room and the hostess's gown but the food itself. Triangular shapes (often quite low) were favourites, with cut ferns, fruits, grasses, and richly-coloured flowers often included. Flowers under glass domes, and hand posies made in concentric rings around a central flower, are very much of this age.

149

Pinholders

A pinholder is a flat, heavy piece of metal into which rows of strong pins are embedded. It can be used in conjunction with chicken wire in a deep container, or alone in a shallow container, to support the main vertical stems. Stems are impaled directly on to it and are held at any angle. Some have pins more widely spaced than usual; these have been specially designed to hold flower foams securely.

It is a mistake to use flower foam with a normal pinholder, because it will clog the pins. A good collection of variously sized pinholders is useful, for obviously a small or lightweight one will not support a large number of stems without tipping forward. A well-pinholder comes complete with a built-in dish, or well, for water, and is an invaluable aid in many arrangements, for it is easily hidden by plant material. All types can be bought at florists' shops and flower clubs.

In an emergency a pinholder can be used as a counter-balance for an arrangement in danger of falling forward. Either hook its pins on to the back of the tilting pinholder, or into the chicken wire at the back of the container. This should redress the balance.

Pot-et-fleur

This is the name arrangers give to collections of growing plants put together in a container with cut flowers added. No extra leaves are included, other than those which happen to be on the stems of the flowers. Small water containers are used for the cut flowers and these can usually be easily hidden among the growing plants. Moss, stones, driftwood and suitable accessories may be included to good effect. Pot-et-fleur can be large and splendid – big enough for a grand hall – or small and pretty for the home. Delightful groupings can be achieved with a little thought as to overall harmony of colour and by selecting plants which have contrasting textures and leaf shapes.

Preserving leaves

Many foliages can be preserved by standing the stem ends in a shallow drink made up of two parts hot water to one part glycerine, stirred well together. Sprays of foliage such as beech, camellia, mahonia and ivy can be treated in this way. First prune

away any excess leaves along the branches, and any damaged leaves. Split open and scrape stem ends, and leave them to drink in the mixture until there is a change in the leaf colour, showing that the process is complete. This may take several weeks. Heavier leaves can be preserved in the same mixture if completely submerged in it (fatsia and bergenia, for instance), while others such as aspidistra and rubber plant may be rubbed over with the solution, on both sides of the leaf, from time to time during the shallow drink treatment.

After preservation the foliage can be arranged in water with fresh flowers, but first coat the base of the stems with nail varnish or spray-on paint to prevent mildew. Glycerined foliage may be kept from year to year, and can be washed by swishing it through water containing a little detergent.

Foliage can also be preserved by ironing. Virginia creeper, for example, picked and ironed, when changing red, keeps this colour. Yellowing bracken, green ferns, or tan-coloured sycamore leaves picked up from where they have just fallen, are also ideal for ironing. Collect the leaves on a dry day and press on both sides with a fairly hot iron; the iron must not be so hot as to scorch or char the leaves. You need an old cloth to protect your ironing board, but the leaves themselves need no protection from the iron. Iron right over each leaf but try not to break the ribs. After ironing, place the leaves flat under a heavy book until all the moisture has really dried out. These ironed leaves are much more brittle than those preserved by the glycerine process, and so need to be carefully handled.

Preserving plant material

There are many ways of preserving plant material nowadays – by direct heat, by hanging up to dry, pressing, spray painting, the glycerine method, or using a drying medium, while some plant material dries off naturally by itself in the garden or when brought indoors. Flowers and foliage to be preserved should be picked when absolutely dry and at perfection.

Hanging to dry

Stems of delphinium, bunched achillea, Chinese lanterns, larkspur, statice and other suitable material can be hung above a radiator or kitchen boiler, or in the airing cupboard, where they will quickly dry, keeping a good colour.

Heat preservation

Place flowers such as mature hydrangea, late double roses, delphinium, and hosta leaves, in shallow water in a container and then stand the container on a radiator or in the airing cupboard, and the flowers and leaves will dry beautifully. The hostas twist and turn into strange tan-coloured shapes as they dry. Late roses, zinnias, and other sturdy flowers will often dry well if placed directly on a warm radiator out of water. Gather the heads of helichrysum (the stems are hardly worth preserving) before the flowers show the colour of their eyes, and leave them to dry in a warm place 151

(I use a cake cooling tray in the airing cupboard). The blooms can be dried just as they are for calendar and picture making, but if you want stemmed flowers for an arrangement press a florists' wire, turned over at the top to form a hook, right down through the centre of the flower; the hook keeps the wire stem in place. The wire can be covered with brown or green gutta-percha tape or a ribbon of crepe paper.

Drying mediums

Special drying mediums usually contain silica gel, which can be bought in the less satisfactory crystal form from the larger branches of Boots (I find the hard crystals pock-mark tender petals). A good brand-named agent is Lastingflower. Silica gel preserves flowers of all seasons, and their stems, perfectly, with every petal holding its contours, every stamen erect, from the first buttercups and daisies to late 'button' chrysanthemums. Huge blooms such as the mop-headed chrysanthemums, or flowers which have large bell or trumpet shapes, like lilies and orchids, are not however suitable. The lifespan of material preserved in silica gel can be lengthened by spraying with matt poster paint, pastel fixative, or hair lacquer; this also brings up the colour of material which seems too dried-looking. The slight glow gives the effect of china flowers, which you may like. To use a drying agent, cover the bottom of a plastic box or a tin with about one inch of the medium and place the flowers on it, face up. Trickle more of the medium carefully round the flowers until they are covered. Make sure

every crevice is filled and the blooms are supported by the drying medium. More layers of flowers and medium may be added, but the final layer must be the drying agent.

Spray painting

Painting a fresh pink or carnation bloom, a rosebud, a head of wallflower or stock, or a spray of ivy, with car body spray-on paint is a method of instant preservation which produces the effect of porcelain flowers. Spray the blooms lightly all over, making a number of passes rather than applying one heavy coat, and make sure to get the paint right down between the petals. The exact living shape of each flower, leaf, berry or bract is immediately preserved for ever as the paint excludes air. The colours do tend to fade after a year or so, but a quick re-spray enables the flowers and leaves to go on for many years. They look delightful arranged in fine china containers which have similar painted flower decoration. In choosing spray paints, pick colours as near as possible to the natural hues of the material you wish to treat, or else select colours to match the decor of your room. To create real works of art, you can then hand-paint the veining, etc, of the plant material with a fine brush and poster paints, finishing with clear varnish spray.

Pressing flowers and leaves

You can buy special flower presses, or make your own with a 'sandwich' of blotting paper between two pieces of hardboard, weighted with bricks or heavy books.

R

Reel and stub wires

Florists' reel wire and stub wires are both important to flower arrangers. Stub wires come in various thicknesses; the standard gauges go from sixteen, which is the strongest, to thirty, which is the finest.

Fine reel wire is used for a variety of purposes, including securing chicken wire in a container, attaching florists' tubes to sticks, and such jobs as binding plant material to ropes, when making swags. If you only need a small amount, a card of household fuse wire may fill the bill.

Stub wires are used for making artificial stems for dried flowers (disguised with florists' gutta-percha tape), and as emergency splints for broken stems. Weak hollow stems will often take a strengthening stub wire, but wired stems in an arrangement of fresh plant material will, unless skilfully done, tend to assume odd and unnatural angles.

Rocks, stones and pebbles

Flower arrangers are accustomed to using driftwood, yet designs featuring rocks and shapely stones accompanied by flowers, leaves, or growing plants, are rare. Stones are seen in a secondary role, simply covering up the mechanics of an arrangement, acting as accessories, or adding a little visual weight, but they can have a higher purpose. Instead of simply being accessories they can take a really prominent part in, say, an oriental-inspired flowerpiece or landscape. These can certainly look dramatic as window-ledge decorations, with large pierced and pitted sea shore rocks seen in silhouette, with a few tall, slim backing leaves perhaps, and the flowers grouped low in the design.

The best of English rockeries use handsome stones against which flowers are seen to exceedingly good effect. A few large, interesting and shapely rocks, scaled down to homely size and placed on a flat dish, an old tray, a big plate, or a fabric-covered base can be grouped to take a dominant part in a design, and will make handsome settings for flowers and leaves. One or two well-pinholders or a small block of Oasis for the cut stems can be easily hidden among or behind the stones; small pot plants, or tiny growing ferns, might also play a part. Driftwood marries very well into rock designs.

The colours and markings of a stone are enhanced when it is damp or is seen through water, and the same effect can be gained by varnishing; this is usually most successful with smooth water-worn stones. I have often painted stones in soft smudgy colours to get a particular effect, and I find that using a dappling of several colours is best for a natural look.

Low, handleless baskets filled with big round sea-washed pebbles can make original settings for winter-day designs of dried flowerheads, and try a tall classically-shaped container in which just a few dramatic flower stems cut to varying heights, are arranged on a pinholder, surrounded by gravel or 153

suitable sea-smoothed stones. Designs need not necessarily be naturalistic; interesting modern and abstract effects are possible when stones are presented like pieces of modern sculpture, selected, of course, with an eye to their general harmony and the happy interplay of textures, colours, and forms.

Split flints, showing their intricate inner markings or hollow inner shapes can often be picked up by the sea, or at the roadside in gravel areas. Limestone country yields shales and ancient weathered rocks sometimes carrying moss or lichen; quartz and similar semi-precious stones can often be found in shell shops at the seaside. Coal comes in good shapes or can be split, and is interesting when used with red, orange, white or soft yellow flowers.

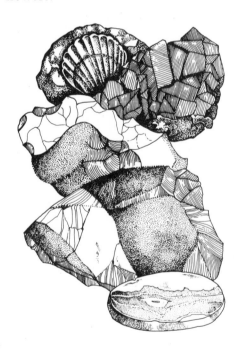

Show schedules

The schedule for a flower arrangement show contains a list of the classes, the show rules, and details such as times for staging and time of judging. The whole schedule, including the general rules, should be read with care and must be strictly followed by all competitors. If the show is to be judged by a qualified NAFAS judge it is vital to read the schedule in conjunction with the current NAFAS *Handbook of Schedule Definitions* (obtainable through flower arrangement clubs, and from NAFAS). Both exhibitor and judge have to adhere to the schedule and the Handbook, although it should be remembered that the individual schedule takes precedence over the Handbook. (See also page 102.)

Those drawing up schedules should remember 'the simpler the better'. In particular try not to have classes asking for very specific things such as 'flowers and leaves only', in a class entitled 'Autumn', for example, this would mean no arranger could include seasonal berries. Such schedules may be fun to write but are less fun to interpret – no wonder that would-be exhibitors are sometimes put off.

T

Table decorations

Although arrangements for tables at home will often be informal, this does not mean that they should lack interest and not be pleasantly designed, or that they cannot sometimes even be a bit of fun! When people hear that your hobby is flower arranging it is amazing how often you are called on to help with table flowers for various events.

A show class for a table decoration might ask for 'a formal Victorian dinner table decoration, an exhibit with accessories', 'a luncheon table for two without accessories', or 'a wedding buffet with or without accessories', and so on, so that we become adept at thinking up original and varied themes. Drapes are not usually required (unless the schedule specifically says so) as they would not appear in real situations. Arrangers are usually expected to bring their own table covers, accessories, etc. These obviously should be chosen with care to link with the given theme.

Simple designs in the home can delight the eye. For a breakfast table in the kitchen, three dahlia heads with their own leaves on a cereal plate, a branch of cherry blossom 'growing' among rocks, a gathering of wild roses or wallflowers in a simple jug, are refreshing.

A pineapple set on a frill of laurel or geranium leaves makes a quick and entertaining centrepiece for a winter table, perhaps on a wood base with a

pale apricot, orange, or green cloth or table mats. Choose a pineapple with a good deep rosette of leaves at the top. Cut off the bottom of the fruit so that it will stand firm. Decorate the rosette with a few short-stemmed daisy chrysanthemums, geranium flower-heads, or orange gerberas if you are really pushing the boat out. The rosette will usually hold a little water between the leaves, but in any case well-conditioned flowers will last for an evening and can be restored later by being floated up to their necks in water overnight.

Buffet tables, it is usually suggested, should have arrangements which go soaring upwards, using tall containers such as stemmed pedestal types and candelabra, so that the flowers may be clearly seen above the heads of the guests.

For the large formal party where there are many guests, space is limited and no one sits down, this can be a good idea. But in my experience flowers, fruits, etc, look just as effective when arranged quite low, even among the food itself, or with one or more arrangements rising up from the level 155

of the table. They can be seen quite well and admired as each guest approaches the table. Where guests do not serve themselves, check that the flower arrangements are sufficiently important and can be seen by people sitting down away from the serving table. Individual arrangements for the small tables are usually liked, and here Oasis rounds on plates or saucers with flowers and leaves are invaluable in the case of an outside event, for they can be arranged at home beforehand and quickly set in place 'on the day'. For any table, big and small, the flower arrangement should be in proportion to it and the arranger must remember at the same time to leave sufficient room for place settings, food, coffee cups and so on!

When the dining table is not in use it can hold a really large summer-day design which is beautiful all the way round. Massed table arrangements take much more plant material – and take longer to do. This is where a simpler line arrangement or a very informal bunch design may win on all counts as an everyday table decoration for the busy woman.

Triangles

The triangle-shaped arrangement is always popular, but because all flowers and leaves are different no two triangle arrangements will ever be exactly the same. The asymmetrical triangle sounds frightening, but the term merely means a triangle with sides of irregular, instead of equal, length. Drawing a few different triangles is a quick way of appreciating their possibilites and pleasures.

Vertical arrangements

When space is limited, an arrangement which stresses the vertical line is, like the soaring grace of a church spire, most impressive. Keep it slim and go as high as you dare! Tall containers are valuable here, as they not only aid the feeling of the narrow thrusting shape but also link the flowers and leaves with the container. All naturally spiky flowers, such as gladioli, larkspur, hollyhock and delphinium, lend themselves ideally, for the basic shape of the arrangement repeats their own manner of growth. Some forceful flowers and leaves are needed through the design, to prevent any appearance of dullness or top-heaviness.

Water arrangements

In water arrangements, plant material is often quite sparse – results are usually not so good if any effect of overcrowding occurs. Just one tall and very beautifully shaped branch, such as wisteria, or laburnum in flower, or weeping willow, 'growing' up from pebbles in a wide-mouthed pot, and dripping down over the rim, can be quite moving in its simplicity. Accompanying flowers or foliage at the foot of the branch might seem in the event to be almost unnecessary, but this you must decide at the time. A brief expanse of water can also play a lovely part when using a few flowers low in a shallow natural or pottery shell, and this can be specially useful if your shell has a pretty fluted edge or attractive inner markings which you do not want to hide. Very good on my dining table is a deep oval pewter plate, or three round glass plates set together, with bluebells and their leaves, young beech leaves and small wild flowers arranged in them with the water showing. At home I arrange every sort of flower and leaf in a water arrangement if the plant material looks happy in its setting, but it pays to be careful if using accessories – miniature animals which are clearly land-based look wrong if standing up to their haunches in water!

For show work, much depends on the theme of the class, and hothouse orchids would plainly not be suitable for a class entitled, say, 'By the riverside'. You may smile, but I have seen stranger things in shows.

Water syphoning

Complete a handsome arrangement satisfactorily, top up the water level, and ooze, drip, water begins to syphon down the container and over the table top. It has happened at some time to us all! The culprit is invariably a leaf, a stem, or string holding the chicken wire. Where it touches the rim of the container, it starts to act as a syphon. Locate the trouble and either raise the trouble-maker away from the rim or cut the string and slide it out.

157

INDEX

Numbers in *italics* refer to illustrations

Derbyshire, Jane.
   The flower arrangers' year.